Also by George Economou

Poetry
The Georgics
Landed Natures
Poems for Self-Therapy
Ameriki; Book One and Selected Earlier Poems
Voluntaries
harmonies & fits
Century Dead Center

Translations
Philodemos, His Twenty-Nine Extant Poems
William Langland's Piers Plowman,
          A Verse Translation of the C Version
I've Gazed So Much, Poems by C. P. Cavafy
Acts of Love, Ancient Greek Poetry from Aphrodite's Garden
Half an Hour, Poems by C. P. Cavafy

Criticism
The Goddess Natura in Medieval Literature
Janus Witness: Testament of a Greek American Poet

Editor
Geoffrey Chaucer, A Collection of Original Articles
In Pursuit of Perfection: Courtly Love in Medieval Literature
          (with Joan M. Ferrante)
Proensa, An Anthology of Troubadour Poetry *translated by Paul
          Blackburn*
Poem of the Cid, *translated by Paul Blackburn*

Ananios of Kleitor

Poems & Fragments and Their Reception
from Antiquity to the Present

Collected and translated by

GEORGE ECONOMOU

Shearsman Books
Exeter

Published in the United Kingdom in 2009 by
Shearsman Books Ltd
58 Velwell Road
Exeter EX4 4LD

www.shearsman.com

ISBN 978-1-84861-033-0

Acknowledgements:
Selections from this work have appeared previously in *Golden Handcuffs Review* and
in the published version of The Kimon Friar Lecture in Neo-Hellenic Arts & Letters,
Janus Witness: Testament of a Greek-American Poet (Athens, 2000).

The award of a Fellowship in Poetry by the National Endowment for the Arts in 1999
provided a greatly appreciated opportunity to research and eventually to ascertain,
to the fullest extent possible, the historical contingencies that guided the remarkable
trajectory of the literary career of Ananios of Kleitor.

The poem by Rufinos in this book's Endnotes, p. 104, is reprinted from *Acts of
Love, Ancient Greek Poetry from Aphrodite's Garden* by George Economou, translation
copyright © 2006 by George Economou. Used by permission of Modern Library, a
division of Random House, Inc.

The Papyrus #4922b reproduced on the flyleaf is copyright © The Regents of the
University of Michigan. Image digitally reproduced with the permission of Traianos
Gagos, Archivist, Papyrus Collection, Graduate Library, University of Michigan.

Cover image copyright © Peter Zelei, 2008.

CONTENTS

FOR ROCHELLE

"DAIMONIH,…"

INTRODUCTION

"How could she hear, her ears all stuffed with leaves?"
Daphne (1959)

Once upon a time in Constantinople, a courtier, wishing to pay a supreme compliment to the emperor's mistress as she and her retinue passed by in public, softly spoke the first words, "οὐ νέμεσις (You can't blame)," and nothing more from a passage in the *Iliad* (3.156–58). But it was sufficient for all within earshot to summon the rest of the speech to mind, since they were each and every one immediately familiar with the words that followed, "Trojans and well-greaved Achaians for suffering pain so long for such a woman," and to register with pleasure their approval of the implicit comparison of the beauty of their contemporary royal paramour to that of Helen, "wondrously like the immortal goddesses to look upon." Thirteen centuries separate the source of this story, the *Chronographia*, 6.61, of Michael Psellus (1018–c.1078), and Plato's *Ion*, an elegant little dialogue about the rhapsodic Homeric recitations of the philosopher's day and his dubious view of their ability to contribute anything of value to the understanding of human affairs. Yet there lingers in the Byzantine anecdote the slightest trace of Socrates' famous analogy in the *Ion* of the elements of poetic performance to a magnetic field. While the comparison of the concatenation of divinely inspired poet, rhapsode, and audience to a series of rings held together by a magnetic-like force originally imparted to them by the Muse, is meant to illustrate Plato's view of how the irrational may overpower and possess human nature, the story Michael Psellus tells reveals the cultural synergy of a distinctive literary sophistication that paraded through the cosmopolitan society in which he and his contemporaries lived. It is clearly a very late, if perhaps not the last, faint glimmer we have of a form and practice of literacy that is far removed from that of our own time and ken.

For us, continuity and connection with such poetry must be made through the sweat of our brows. To engage poems as old to us as Homer's were to the Byzantines—indeed older and stranger to our eyes and ears—we must study long and hard. And we must produce leaders in the persons of scholars upon whose individual and collective efforts we are utterly dependent to recover the discourse of past generations from their rare and, at times, intractable physical embodiments, even in the smallest of pieces, artifacts that have fallen prey to the relentless pursuit of random destructive conditions. As W. H. Auden has said as corrective to the patronizing reproach of William Butler Yeats in 'The Scholars', the same poem that inspired Anastas Krebs to emulate his private Catullus in the person of Ananios of Kleitor as he devoted himself to the retrieval of the ancient Greek's poems and fragments during the first half of the twentieth century: "Edit indeed; Thank God they do. If it had not been for scholars working themselves blind copying and collating manuscripts, how many poems would be available, including those of Catullus, and how many others full of lines that made no sense? . . . [O]nly the scholar with his unselfish courage to read the unreadable will retrieve the rare prize."[1]

It was largely due to the efforts of such a scholar, the aforementioned Anastas Krebs of Munich's Ludwig-Maximilians Universität, that Ananios of Kleitor was liberated from one of literary history's most firmly sealed oubliettes. It was a release many years in the coming, which only commenced with the decision of a classicist trained primarily in ancient history and warfare, but who had also mastered a broad range of scholarly competencies, to unveil and ascertain the identity of a poet who had been victimized by a deplorable case of lingering academic negligence. Exactly why, other than for a passionate and abiding love of poetry, did Professor Krebs respond to a call that he pursue the recovery of the poems of a fourth-century BC Ananios, we do not now nor will probably ever know. Nor can we be certain of exactly when he realized that Ananios of Kleitor was a singular poet and person distinct from any other or the ranks of the anonymous, and that his poems had to be differentiated from those of the Ananios of earlier record, the sixth century BC iambographer, to whom a small handful of verses along with the credit for the invention of the ischiorrhogic, or broken-hipped, line have been attributed. We can be sure, however, that the publication in the early 1930s of the commentaries of the Anonymous Alexandrian and Theonaeus constituted a welcome, though by no means indispensable, confirmation of his already well-founded scholarly convictions concerning the poems and fragments of Ananios of Kleitor. It is due to his work, despite the impossibility of our appreciating its full measure, that we now enjoy this addition to the sum of our literary legacy from antiquity.[2]

This legacy comprises the complete extant works contained in this volume, and includes forty-one poetic items, most of them in a fragmentary state, drawn from papyrological sources, and some twenty-five passages of varying length, transcribed from both papyri and medieval codices containing commentaries, conversations, and little disquisitions within whose frames of reference Ananios occupies a significant place. Other than the approximate birth date of 399 BC in the Arcadian city of Kleitor, reported by the Greek author Theonaeus as being proposed by Chamaemelon of Patrae in his lost work on Achaian and Arcadian poets, next to nothing is really known about the life of Ananios. Coming from Kleitor, he must have grown up speaking the dialect known as Arcado-Cyprian, but there is no trace of it in his writing, which shows the usual dialectal mixture of Greek poetry, with West Greek, or Doric, and Attic being the most salient. While we can trust his words to speak for his poetic gifts, we should hesitate, according to one of the imperatives of scholarly tradition, to take them literally concerning his life, though I personally have no serious problems believing the little that he tells us about himself.[3] That this little seems mostly concerned with his amatory life, real or imagined, cannot be denied upon a first reading of his extant lines. But one look is not quite enough to fully take in Ananios, and the numerous other themes and topics that hover alluringly about his words often lead us into a suspended, never to be satisfied state of fascination with his evanescent *logopoieia*, like the delicious aromas wafting from the kitchens of restaurants we are destined to pass but never enter. Because I firmly believe that the reader of these poems and fragments should be allowed a completely free response to them, I will retreat from my inclination to suggest interpretive directives at this point, and end with two brief comments concerning the translation and the annotations I have furnished to assist and enrich what will be for most readers a first and only meeting with Ananios.

In translating these poems and fragments of Ananios of Kleitor into the English of our time, I have attempted to convey his sense as accurately and idiomatically as I can, being committed to making as meaningful a connection as possible with his intelligence, if not with his sensibility, which, belonging to a distant age, eludes our ability to experience it with a clarity that is free of the static interferences generated by the relentless idiosyncrasies of history's course and of our own natures.[4] We hear something, but too many leaves have been turned and fallen between us to hear it all.[5]

Because of the extreme diversity, not to mention density, of the matter in this work, I have chosen to offer my annotations and remarks in the form of running commentaries upon each discrete item and its contents in the hope of making it easier and more rewarding for the reader to consult them after, or even before, every encounter with their referents. That the reader may decide to honor the well-worn practice of skipping them altogether, I am quite aware (with apprehension) and prepared to accept (with disapprobation). But if that should be the case, I would strongly plead against overlooking the *Index Nominum*.

A Note on Spelling

Throughout my translations and commentaries I have followed the practice, with a few exceptions, of using English transliteration for the spelling of Greek names and words. For the sake of accuracy, however, I have allowed the Latinized spellings used by Barker and Sewtor-Lowden to stand. Thus, Ananios of Kleitor, Loussoi, etc. occur as Ananius of Clitor and Lusi, etc. in the texts of these earlier scholars. Like many others, I have abandoned a convention that would spell the name of the poet Alkaios as Alcaeus, and pronounce it, as I have heard individuals with degrees in classics, as "Al-say-us." Similarly, like many who prefer English transliteration, I am disinclined to be obsessively consistent. If "Dionysos" for "Dionysus" is more accurate and unproblematic, "Bakchos" for "Bacchus" looks intolerably odd to me and I retain in its case, as well as in that of a few others, the older, traditional spelling. Alerted thus, the reader should have no difficulty adjusting to this practice.

Notes to the Introduction

[1] *The Dyer's Hand* (New York: Random House, 1962), p.43. Ironically, the same scholars he has defended against Yeats's "libel" and "nonsense" will one day retrieve the poems Auden decided to excise from the body of his work, the best known of which, 'September 1, 1939', he first deprived of its stanza containing the line, "We must love one another or die," on the shaky grounds of his own excessive literalism that we must die anyway, and then, some years later, rejected in its entirety as trash. A poet's puny will to eradicate a poem that has found broad acceptance, as in the case as well of Paul Celan's repudiation of his 'Todesfuge' because it said things better left unsaid, cannot compete with the ruinous accidents visited by time and nature upon the markings with which we bear witness to our passing presence. And yet, as

we persist in our attempts to minimize the consequences and to control the damage of those accidents upon our precious record, we may also find our efforts assisted by unlooked-for strokes of good fortune. Consider the blind luck abetted by human industry that combined to recover and publish in 1974 the celebrated epode by Archilochos known as the Cologne Fragment, despite the stacked odds against a rescue from its languishing state for centuries as mummy-wrapping. If some person with a stronger practical than a poetic bent decided to put an edition of Archilochos' poems to such use rather than tossing it to an uncertain fate into the great dump heap of the Upper Nile, his decision to act thus proved essential to an outcome, albeit enormously belated, that, after all is said and done, was favorable to the cause of poetry. Under such circumstances—and we are—we must expect that attempts like those of Auden and Celan, not to mention that modern Alexandrian C.P. Cavafy, to consign certain of their poems to oblivion are doomed to failure, however much we might sympathize with their mid-twentieth century predicaments. The prison cell in which Melampous heard the worms say it was about to crumble was more secure.

[2] Our perception of Krebs' accomplishment, however, must come mainly through the lens of the only edition we have of Ananios, the one prepared by Sir Michael Sewtor-Lowden and published by William Grossmann of London in 1960. Our other source is the predominantly epistolary account of the events that lead up to the publication of this edition, an account I believe that deserves to be accepted as part of the poet's reception, despite the various troubling questions it raises and its wayward influence upon the trajectory of history. We might have had more secure access to the truth of these and perhaps many other matters had it not been for the disappearance, shortly after the publication of Sewtor-Lowden's edition, of virtually all of the original research materials, including transcriptions and annotations, that Krebs had compiled and collected, an inexplicable and lamentable incident that may have deprived us of some telling clues as to the provenance of this work even as it has most definitely removed from our view the incalculably valuable record of its construction. That Krebs rather impulsively passed these materials into the hands of the young English scholar Jonathan Barker, who in turn permitted them to be unceremoniously appropriated by Sewtor-Lowden, his Cambridge mentor, who then proceeded without compunction to base his edition on them, all bespeak states of academic desperation, albeit of discrepant kinds.

[3] Paradoxically, it turns out that less, not even a birthplace, has been known for centuries about the sixth century iambic poet of the same name, than the precious little we now know of Ananios of Kleitor.

[4] The Greek texts, of course, may be found in *The Poems and Fragments of Ananius of Clitor: An Authoritative Edition Compiled and Annotated, with an Introduction by Sir Michael Sewtor-Lowden* (London: William Grossmann Ltd.,

1960), and in the same scholar's 'Three Poems by Ananius of Clitor', *Review of Classical Studies*, 31 (January, 1953), 46–58).

5 In a marginal addition in the newly discovered manuscript sheets of the first draft of his 1822/1828 lecture 'The Varieties of Historical Writing', Hegel surely is not barking up the wrong tree when he avers that try as we may and must, we finally cannot understand the ancient Greeks any more than "the perceptions of a dog." See *Die Vernunft in der Geschichte*, 13–14; 18, and *Lectures on the Philosophy of World History*, trans. H. B.. Nisbet (Cambridge University Press, 1975), pp.17–18.

ΑΝΑΝΙΟΣ

The Poems & Fragments
of Ananios

1.   ] below Kleitor,

    speckled perch [

         ] in the yellow [

    chirp and [   ] enchantment.

2.   Let go of me my song

    and swoop into the hearts

    of men Love has singed

    and darkened their brightest day.

    Let go of me my song

    and hover between the faces

    [   ]

    your shadows forming letters.

    Return to me my song

    and [

          ] sustain

    my famished [

3.   I will give as good [

by Aphrodite [

[

Either way [

and kiss behind the [

Again [

till it melts [

]turn this [

And again [

your mouth [

Love's mother [

[

On our knees [

breathing each [

4.   She was so black
I called her crow.
She called me back
and called and called
and called. I stopped.

5.   barren [

          ] the beach at Kos [

                                            ]

Phorkys [

         ] such bathing.

6.   of Love's happy captives,

   [   ]

   [

   ] write satisfaction

in my heart to [

         ] desires.

7.   To you, Aphaia, I cry, I [

                   ] Hear,

O, hear me now that [

                                    ]

Can it be the invisible [

8.   As the shepherd tilts his ear into the wind
to catch the lost lamb's bleating, so [

9.   ] remember

    to honor Athena [

             ] started back in surprise [

                        ] breath

                        taking.

[   ] like [Eu]ryale's

    echoing wail [

                  ] favorite flute-girl

    for melodies Apollo heard the satyr make.

10. Yet the wild bull may be led to sacrifice

    if the priestess can tie a fig branch round his neck.

11.   Dance through the forest [   ] deer season (cakes?) [

             Artem]is shouts and shoots [

    as the moon [   ] on flying feet [

               ] the precipice

   ] fisherman's net [   ] my heart, my love [

12.   ] a pro from Corinth,

a honey-voiced [

who rides me like a pony [

Aphrodite the Dark [

on her billy-goat [

A philosopher would say it's [   ] h⟨uma⟩n.

13.   Sweet dreams [
                    ] sunbeams [
                            ] of me.

14.   ] enough time [

15.   [Th]ucydides measures the Attic war's
            first eight-and-a-half years by the tenure
            as priestess at Argos' temple of He[ra
            of Ch]rysis, who fell asleep and let it
            catch fire, then awoke and fled in the night.
            She was old, and you, much less than half her age,
            what's your excuse, Pyrrha, for the havoc
            you have made of my life in just three months?

16.   Pyrrha, perhaps you'd be
       [   ]
       if this were the old me
       instead of the old me.

17.   Of the three girls I loved this year,
       I cut off the third, vain little Xantho,
       who refused to play the flute for me
       because it would distort her face,
       and for that severance I paid dearly.
       Now when I see her in the street,
       she grimaces and hisses, even spits
       my way and dooms me by this music
       to look away from her wild eyes
       and bit by bit my heart to turn to stone.

18.   Melampous overheard the worms overhead

19.   ] the suitors, loud and [
              ] playing pebbles [
                     ] another man's [
                        ] luck [

20. Quick, savor what the gods give you.
    There's something behind you, baring its teeth.

21. black broth they drink in Sparta

22. while making love we passed an olive

23. the thrill is

24. Aphrodite, the shapely, fills me

25. lips that cry for wine

26. in the dark, her castanets

27. the most beautiful time

28. Chrysosastros took a flop
    last night as he left the brothel.
    Pity for him blows in me
    as on a small flute.

29a.   where I intend to make out like a Corinthian

29b.   after she plays the flute for me, I'll devour my Anchovy

30. Laïs tells why she rolled with you for free:
         Can a dog be expected to pay rent?

31.   ] feeble strand [
                                    ] oh [
                           ] mark of [
                           ] contrivance
                           ]
                           ] yawning [
                           ]
                           ] shame on your Schadenfreude.

32.   he'll go since what is fated cannot be fled

33.   old friend, I'll bring a cabbage for your pot

34.   ] daughter(s?) [
                                    ] Proitos (Proteus?) [
                                              ] savior [

35.   ] astonishing in sunlight [

                            ] the price of Eros [

                                ] then she gave it [

36.   ] outstanding, upstanding breasts [

37.   ]

                    ] cows no more

                        ] the waters [

38.   [

                    ]

             divine figs for all [

             [

             [   ] aftertaste of sweet almonds [

                            ] back and forth [

                    ] far from the seaside[

                                    ] star gazing and crazy.

39.   Melite's can be played like Hermes' lyre,

             up front and down back with equal sweetness.

40. [   ] of all my words [

     [

     [   ] O Aphrodite [

     [

     if I could touch [

     [

     "despair" carved in the rock face by the Styx

     [

     [

     still it comes [   ] after Persephone's

     summer with Hades and [

41.   ] awe [

                                     ] none [

                                       ] oh, yes [

THE RECEPTION

ANCIENT, MEDIEVAL & MODERN

THE ANONYMOUS ALEXANDRIAN

1. On the *Iliad* 13.227, "perish unpraised": Ananios, perhaps following Euripides' *Rhesus* 751, "But we die without honor or purpose," as well, writes:

> honored too late for deaths without purpose

2. On the *Odyssey* 5.85, "Calypso, lustrous goddess": This is an epithet Ananios of Kleitor uses in a light-hearted, playful way:

> show yourself, my lustrous girl

3. On the *Odyssey* 5.28, "struck and killed him with his bright thunder-bolt": While Homer shows how Zeus punished Iasion for sleeping with Demeter in the thrice-plowed fallow field, Ananios says that he will avoid such punishment:

> As long as I stay away from goddesses and country girls,
> no bright thunder-bolts will shoot out of the blue at me.

4. On the *Odyssey* 11.123, "never seasoned with salt": Compare to this the line by Ananios:

> death in a grove seasoned with pine not salt

5. On the *Odyssey* 19.91, "brazen, shameless bitch": Ananios uses this phrase in the following manner:

> Melantho, what drew me to you,
> you brazen, shameless bitch,
> now makes me want to draw away.

6. On Apollonius of Rhodes *Argonautica* 3.120, "mad love": by metonymy, "love that makes mad," as in Ananios:

> reckless love

7. On the *Iliad* 21.493-4, "fled in tears as a pigeon in flight from a hawk": several poets, including Hermesianax and Ananios, have used this simile. The latter writes:

> and you fled from Hera as a pigeon flies from a hawk

8. On the *Odyssey* 20.355, "full of ghosts is the porch and the court": Ananios of Kleitor ends a poem about the suitors with this line:

> ghosts he who sprang from Melampous' line called them.

9. On Pindar *Pythian* 12.30, "what is fated cannot be avoided": Here at the end of this ode in praise of Midas of Acragas, who won the flute playing competition at Delphi despite a broken mouthpiece, Pindar says a god may give or withhold unexpected success. Ananios of Kleitor uses this same expression in one of his poems.

10. On Sappho, "more finely shaped": Ananios of Kleitor also uses this in a comparison between two young women, though I have not found in any other poet but him the word *orthotitthon* (ὀρθότιτθον),

> erect of breast

which he uses in the same poem.

11. On the *Iliad* 24.130-32, wherein Thetis, warning Achilles that his days are numbered, urges him to take pleasure in sleeping with a woman, saying it would be a good thing: Aristarchos, our great librarian, rejects these verses, though Ananios of Kleitor honors them in one of his poems:

> only the best of mothers would so advise a son

THEONAEUS

1. *Games for Dinnertime* 2.30: Ananios of Kleitor wrote a hymn to Artemis, if we can believe Chamaemelon of Patrae in his book on the poets of Achaia and Arcadia. I will quote for you what he gives of it:

> Riding a chariot drawn by yoked, tame deer,
> your priestess follows the grand procession,
> all in your honor, all in your remembrance.
> At dawn they will light the pyre before your altar
> and offer you their birds, their boars, their deer,
> and even bear cubs, all burnt whole for you,
> whose wondrous temple at Ephesus has burned
> to ashes, whose ears Hera laughingly
> spanked with your own bow on the Trojan plain.

Chamaemelon explains that Ananios, who traveled to Corinth regularly in order to visit the Temple of Aphrodite, has written these lines as a way of showing that he respects Artemis less than he does her great rival. Since he came from Kleitor, he could have easily journeyed to Patrae, where Artemis is worshipped, and to Corinth, to witness in each city the splendid festival held in honor of its goddess. Others say Ananios often nourishes his verse by including stories like Homer's tale of Hera's scolding of Artemis. Some say Ananios seldom, if ever, left the precincts of Kleitor, where Chamaemelon says he was born during the Nemean Crown Games following the 95th Olympiad, while others claim he left as a young man, living in Corinth and Athens, and never returned.

2. *Games for Dinnertime* 3.18 [on flutes]: Ananios of Kleitor speaks of small flutes, called by some half-bores because they have half the usual number of holes and stops, when he complains to his friend and fellow poet, Chrysosastros:

> You seem to think, my friend, you can play me
> like a flute, know my stops, my every note,
> though you can't even pipe a musical
> toodle-doo on the simplest of half-bores.

3. *Games for Dinnertime* 3.20 [on flutes]: Once at dinner, I heard my friend Alkimides read a poem by Ananios in which the poet described the angry face of a lover he jilted because she would not play the flute for him. I was reminded of Plutarch's account of how Marsyas tried to modify the ugly puffing out of his face when he played the flute by wearing cheekbands. But Alkimedes insisted she was offended by the poet's attempt to put her into the role of a two-bit (*didrachmon* [δίδραχμον]) flute-girl (*auletris* [αὐλητρίς]). Later, I remembered and related to our company that this is the same poem that Chamaemelon says brings to mind the time in the forest of Mount Ida when Athena invented the flute but threw it away in disgust after she played it and saw reflected in the water of a spring how swollen and ugly it made her face. Where upon Iasios Lakon reminded us that that hand-clapping critter Marsyas promptly picked up the instrument and claimed it for his own. The Spartan doctor then asked us if we understood why Apollo flayed Marsyas alive after hanging him on a pine tree, and we all offered the usual answers that it was because of the satyr's *hubris* in his ridiculous challenge to a musical contest with the god of music and also for his *hubris* in taking what was never meant for him and perhaps for his vain attempt to retain his looks while playing the flute as well. But Iasios Lakon insisted that Apollo, after trading with baby Hermes for his lyre and Pan-pipes, having heard Marsyas play the flute, realized the power of that playing could charm the souls of mortals and immortals too, even as to this day such melodies, whether played through the breathing of a master or a common flute-girl, possess a power over men no other has, and Apollo thus desired to possess it also for himself. Knowing he would fail to take Marsyas' treasure through the musical competition alone, he resolved to capture the powers of his flute by resorting to a womanish trick and turned his own instrument upside down and played it and then challenged the satyr to do the same with his, which was impossible. Having thus attained his first desire, Leto's son carried out the cruel sentence he had planned for Marsyas by getting him to agree earlier that the victor could impose whatever punishment he wished upon the vanquished and tore his skin from his living body. The sight of this bleeding, inflamed, pulsating trophy allowed the new music to enter Apollo's eyes and he was possessed by an intense and dangerous pleasure by its full manifestation in him when next he played upon his lyre.

4. *Games for Dinnertime* 4.6: Kteson, who hails from Ithaca, explained to me the kind of game the suitors played as they sat in Odysseus' doorway [17.530–531]: After dividing into two sides, they placed a pebble, which they called Penelope, in the middle and cast their own pebbles at her, he who was able to hit Penelope with his own piece twice without touching any other player's piece being declared the winner and given high hopes of marrying her. By occupying themselves with such games, the suitors' arms became so weak and flabby they had little chance of stretching the bow.

Ananios of Kleitor must have heard a similar account, for in one of his poems he describes their folly and then says:

> But I, when it comes to taking down a woman,
> leave nothing to the imagination, or to chance.

5. *Games for Dinnertime* 4.44: Ananios of Kleitor, according to Chamaemelon, once tried to provoke the philosopher Diogenes when he met him in Corinth and was summarily dismissed:

> I heard you went to some lengths, greater even than
> those expended on your poems, to hump the statue of
> Phryne. You're way too fancy for a handyman like me.

6. *Games for Dinnertime* 5.101: I myself held forth at dinner on the by now commonplace figure from Nestor's exhortation to Diomedes, "on a razor's edge stand life and death" [*Iliad* 10. 173-74], explaining how this has been repeated by Herodotus, Theocritus, and many others, including Ananios, who uses it, however, to express the delicately balanced likelihood of success or failure in a new love affair:

> What is the lover's fate? An armful of passion?
> Hands on his own chest? It stands on a razor's edge.

7. *Games for Dinnertime* 6.32: Once again at dinner, Alkimedes recited the poem by Ananios about Xantho, who wouldn't play the flute for him. Making a great show of his learning, he said that the last part of the poem, in which Ananios cuts her, the third of three lovers, off, and her angry gaze then dooms his feelings for her to turn to stone, reminded him, on the one hand, of Pindar's account of Perseus cutting off the head of Medusa and giving it to Polydectes [*Pythian* 12.11–16], but, on the other, just as easily of Hesiod [*Theogony* 280–81 or *Shield of Heracles* 216ff.], or for that matter of the scholiast's comments on Homer's *Iliad* [14.320], in the place where Zeus abjures all his other loves, including Perseus' mother Danaë, in his plea to Hera to bed down with him. But he had nothing further to say after Kteson and I assured him we had also read this in Chamaemelon.

8. *Games for Dinnertime* 7.69 : Of Ananios of Kleitor's poem that begins:

> Bird of ill omen, are you the woman
> the edge of whose garment I fear to touch?

I once heard Iasios Lakon say that it speaks of a kind of commerce between the living and the dead. When I asked this physician from Sparta what, then, was the nature of the pollution that Ananios feared, he sighed and walked away.

9. *Games for Dinnertime* 7.13: Though Chamaemelon seems unaware of the strange things Linos and Epimenides the Cretan wrote about the river Styx, he gives us a four stanza poem by Ananios about "Arcadian Waters," as he [Chamaemelon] calls it, the first of which refers to the Styx. I will quote the entire poem here, just as I read it a few days ago to our gathering of friends:

> Having stood weak-kneed beneath the high crag
> of the Styx's sheer falls above Nonakris,
> I wouldn't, for the life of me, drink a drop of it,
> scooped in a horse's hoof from its Phenean stream below.
>
> The shockingly cold water from Alyssos,
> spring nearby the artless, cruel Kynaithaians' town,
> that cures the mad dog's bite—I can do
> without as well, unless a mad dog bite me.

Also, I'm afraid, my liberty loving Kleitor's
fountain, so delicious its drinker forever
loses his taste for wine; for the doctor
Melampous sang to it and dipped it with hellebore.

No, I'll walk to Lykouria's springs of Ladon,
on whose banks Apollo and Leukippos loved Daphne,
for the best of waters, neat, or better yet
in five parts to two of a fine wine from Chios.

Now because I also read Chamaemelon's note that Ananios says a horse's
hoof on account of its being the only substance from pottery to gold that
can withstand the destructive powers of Styx's water, Kimon, a relative
newcomer to our parties, informed us that Sappho of Mytilene says in
a poem that gold is indestructible and not subject to rust; whereupon
Kteson replied that everyone knows that poem and that the Lesbian was
not concerned with the Styx in it. Kimon then began to say something
about Thetis dipping the infant Achilles in it, to which Kteson gave a
loud laugh, but I interrupted all this with my order for the refreshments
to be served.

★

KOSMAS LOGOTHETES

1. *Recipes for Rhetoric 34*: Another example of *anadiplosis* may be found in
the pagan poet Ananios:

> May Charis' drink ever be fruit of the vine's juice; juice
>   of its leaf never.

Numerous verses of this poet, like those of many other authors of
his time, are conducive to sinful thoughts and acts, yet they are not
without benefit to one who would read them in the spirit of a Christian
upbringing. Observe that Ananios opposes the aphrodisiacal power of
wine with that of the power of the vine leaf's juice to annul it. In this

latter, he is confirmed by Dioscorides, who recommends the leaf's juice as an anaphrodisiac when he says, "To drink the juice of the leaves helps the dysenterical, the blood spitters, and women with unusual yearnings." Although, the poet's words show his dread of the antidotal drink's possible effect upon his mistress, these same words teach us, should we need it, to use a property of nature to resist sin and promote virtue. And further, when we remember the words of Paul to the Romans that all that was written earlier was written for our instruction, we may understand, even through a poet like Ananios, that the plant of God's love gives us both the drink of His Grace and a recipe as well whereby we may quell the carnal love that makes us unworthy to imbibe it. Thus, what the Holy Spirit has inspired in this single line of pagan verse overwhelms utterly any praise such as that given Ananios by the rhetor Xydis of Corinth for his wordplay on *poton* (ποτόν) "drink," *pote* (ποτέ), "ever," and *oudepote* (οὐδέποτε), "not ever," in this line.

2. *Recipes for Rhetoric* 39: We find *antonomasia* in a poem by Ananios when he addresses a friend not by his name but in this way:

> Come here, my fish-mad-man and girl-crazy-guy

We learn later that it is his friend, Chrysosastros, whom he addresses as *opsomanis* (ὀψομᾰνῆς) and gynaikomanis (γυναικομανής), but we learn nothing of spiritual value from such as this, which serves merely to provide us with examples of rhetorical practice for, with the help of the Holy Spirit, our better use.

3. *Recipes for Rhetoric* 69: Concerning further examples of *metaphora*, many who have written about whores use the nickname "Anchovy" to describe such a woman among them who is thin, of light complexion, and has large eyes; it should come as no surprise to us that a poet like Ananios of Kleitor would find this as irresistible a locution to describe one of his paramours as we find the word untalented to describe him.

4. *Recipes for Rhetoric* 88: If you seek an example of *homoiosis*, you may find it, at peril of your immortal soul, in the first of two lines, which Ananios meant to insert into the middle of a poem, worse even than his, by Rufinos, famous for his supposed judging in beauty contests over the private parts of loose women:

> Melite's can be played like Hermes' lyre

What Ananios says may be done with what lies between Melite's thighs in the next verse, it is my sacred obligation to keep to myself.

5. *Recipes for Rhetoric* 119: An example of *zeugma*, if little else of worth, may be found in a poem by Ananios:

> Not goat ribs, nor the seven-leafed cabbage
> by which I swear, can this hangover cure.

It should come as no surprise that this poet sought relief from his vinous overindulgence, *oinophlygia* (οἰνοφλυγία)

> For I have overdrunk this night before.

by such a useless concoction of scapegoat and cabbage. That he and others of his kind believed in the power of cabbage to alleviate the painful price they paid for their immoderate consumption of unmixed wine, *akratos* (ἄκρᾱτος), may be seen in the lines from another of his poems:

> When you come, Chrysosastros, to party tonight,
> Don't forget the cabbages for our morning rite.

The intemperance of his living, along with his excessive attachment to this friend and companion in uncontrolled, *akratos* (ἀκρᾱτῶς), conduct, if I may show my own ability to play with a word (may the Lord forgive my vanity), is epitomized by the silly oath he takes in expressing his unmeasured affection for this person:

> especially of all the people
> I love you the most, by the cabbage.

Let this kind of blasphemy and impurity, which comes far from steering a middle course even in terms of a pagan code of conduct, signify for us the unregenerate state of our human nature before the Savior took it upon Himself in order to save us from it. Ananios, Chrysosastros, and their pot of cabbage must burn in hell. You and I need not.

★

Theophanes

1. *The Holy Book of Accounts (Codex Vaticanus Moreanus)*: As you well know, brethren, our pagan forebears were possessed by an excessive appetite for fish, lost souls that they were and are for all ages. This crazed fish eating, *opsophagia* (ὀψοφᾰγία), which some of them pursued beyond moderation or reason, others of them ridiculed, especially the poets, as does the one called Ananios. But ever the hypocrite, in another place he urges the consumption of various fishes in season, the swordfish and grunting chromios in spring, tuna, outstanding in sauces, and best of all the small shrimp devoured off a fig leaf. They knew not how to eat for their higher sustenance, as do we, the better Greeks that we are by our faith in the One true Father and His "only begotten Son and Word of God," as Justinian hymns. Yes, we are the better Greeks for it. What is that to you, grim faced rock? Or to you, goat-headed sinner? What is that to you, I say again, that the fish, *ICHTHYS* (ΙΧΘΥΣ), upon which we feed is none other than Jesus Christ, God's Son, our Savior, not flesh of a fish *opsarion* (ὀψάριον) sizzling on a fire of coals, which men, believing they need it to live too often find death in it instead and sizzle themselves eternally over the fiery coals of hell. But we eat our life eternal and are become a manner of fish ourselves following Him, who has hooked us with His love, upon the dry land until the day we come into heaven. Let it be known that this is put down in my holy book of accounts and that nothing escapes my eyes and ears. No. Nothing. Not the tearing apart now of the great fish of our faith by you who so mistook St. Peter's sign when, in the name of Jesus Christ, he made the sardine hanging in a window into a living fish and to swim in the bath so that you threw bread to it, O misguided Romans, believing it was for you to feed it rather than to be fed by it yourselves, O worse than our fish-frenzied pagans, and

fattened it with your foul worldly nourishments into a monstrous fish that would devour all the other faithful fishes in its path. O Ichthyophagi, you rip and chew upon the body of our Lord Himself, and she whose name says life but signifies darkness, destruction, and death, she who never gave life has thrown the fish of life to you as if it were scraps from her table. This I, Theophanes, say. I, whom she sent with my master Monomachos into exile, am become the father of this holy hermitage and accountant of the misdeeds of her evil days, I, whom my earthly lord Monomachos deserted after he succumbed to her temptation, am become the way and the voice through which our Lord God may be known in this ancient land of Pelops and the mulberry.

2. *The Holy Book of Accounts (Codex Vaticanus Moreanus)*: Brethren, because I landed beside Corinth in Paul's footsteps and came into that church that is in the house of Akilas and Priska from which the apostle sends his greetings till the breaking of time, the fish scales having fallen from his eyes upon his baptism by that man devout according to the law, Ananias, I have been blessed with the power to read the letters that ride upon the air overhead, invisible to you, but conveying to me in all systems of writing keys to the past and signs of things to come. Because Paul admonishes us to part company with fornicators, idolaters, adulterers, sodomites and the effeminate, I, as it is my appointed turn, now admonish you to put aside all things that may undo your hard won virtue and weigh you down with sin again, even as that Philadelphia, unto the angel of whose church John wrote of his love from Patmos, later returned to its pagan abominations and came, as it well deserved, to be called Little Athens. Revert you not to your Corinthian ways, which you need not be in Corinth for them to lead you to drink from the cup and partake of the table of demons. For Theophanes saw them there and sees them here in the Holy Hermitage, hovering over the heads of his brethren, batting and twisting the letters that do their evil bidding into the ears and eyes of the brethren, whose immortal souls they tempt unto corruption utterly. Yet he who sees all this to put it down in his holy book of accounts, the Lord God's gift to him in recompense for the pain Life/Zoë (?) has brought him, has been granted this visionary power because he faced down the demon that came to him when he had first come into Corinth, saying Ananias am I, the fourth and last and best. See how I make poems

of coming to Corinth to make out like a Corinthian and to listen to a flute girl before I devour my anchovy. I welcome you and bid you open yourself to the enchantments of my poems, which, like the singing fish of Arcadia, may bring you pleasures immeasurable. But he, the Father of this Holy Hermitage, cried out to the vile fish-eating demon, I have seen Ananias, I have known Ananias, Ananias you are not. Unless you be he whose heart Satan filled to lie to the Holy Ghost. Still some will fail to see this in times to come, though I have the power to write your true name, for all its falseness, with a simple wave of my hand through the air, which I now do, transforming alpha into omicron and shifting the fall of the acute to the antepenult. After he had done this, Theophanes made haste to drink from the cup and partake of the table of the Lord. Thus did I cleanse my soul of its contamination by that hypocrite poet Ananios through communion with my Savior and cleared the damning taste of his fishy verses from my lips. Therefore, my brethren, you will no longer keep hold of those books that I know you pore over secretly in your cells, gripping pleasure in your loins from the exquisite sting of their letters in your eyes and their siren ringing in your ears, and surrender them all unto me for your safekeeping from their mad dog bite, against which no waters prevail but only the sacrament I alone am empowered to dispense here, lest you turn by such reckless reading unwittingly into fleshy fishes and find yourselves quite suddenly and irrevocably surprised by your fins. This is to say, my brethren, you shall lose the form and semblance of your Christian manhood like those who came before you and fell into these rocks, birds, goats, and other dumb beasts among us, but you will splash into the rivers no fisher of men but I any longer casts his nets in, and your souls, like those deposited here in nature's prison, will remain its sin-spotted captives forever unless I take pity on you upon the advent of the new Odysseus to reclaim his kingdom and to redeem his faithful servants and destroy the sinful suitors.

*

SEWTOR-LOWDEN

[The three translations below are based on the texts first published by Sir Michael Sewtor-Lowden in 'Three Poems by Ananius of Clitor',

Review of Classical Studies, 31 (January, 1953), 46-58. The Greek texts are preceded in the journal by a short "Introductory Note," which I quote in its entirety.]

The author of these poems, Ananius of Clitor, should not be confused with the sixth-century iambographer of the same name whose handful of surviving fragments are closely associated with the writings of Archilochus and Hipponax. Born early in the fourth-century, perhaps in the year 399, this Ananius produced a considerable body of work, as evidenced by papyrus rolls and fragments of various provenance brought from Egypt since the late 1700s to the great library collections in the British Museum, Oxford, Berlin, and Munich, among others. Though the relative recentness of interest in him may well be due to a long-standing failure to distinguish definitively between him and his earlier namesake, we now, thanks to the industrious gathering of papyrus sources by the late Anastas Krebs of Munich, can no longer overlook his contribution to our legacy from Greek civilization. These restorations constitute the first step towards the preparation of a full edition of the poems of Ananius of Clitor to which my assistant, Dr. Hugh Sydle, and I have committed ourselves.

[As the Ladon runs] below Kleitor,
speckled perch [shimmer and
shimmy] in the yellow [flecked waters,]
chirp and [complete my] enchantment.

＃

I will give as good [as I get, I swear]
by Aphrodite [and her cunning son.
Let them set fire to you first, or to me.]
Either way [the flames will stir us to lick]
and kiss behind the [knees, inside the ears.]

Again [I will swear by their radiant heat]
till it melts [our limbs and lives into one.
Let's] turn this [trick of theirs to our advantage.]
And again [by our submission I swear]
your mouth [and mine will join us at the heart.
Love's mother [and Love himself will not care
as long as we pay the passage with ourselves.]
On our knees [face to face, solid as a herm,]
breathing each [other's breath, cool to the touch.]

#

[Who's to blame I fell for] a pro from Corinth,
a honey-voiced, expensive [smooth-shaven cunt],
who rides me like a pony [in a race she has to win?]
Aphrodite the Dark, [that's who, who climbs the night sky]
on her billy-goat [and lays claim to the world below.]
A philosopher would say it's a matter entirely (human).
                                        or (foolish).
                                                or (useless).

[Readers who wish to consult the copious, verging on the prolix, textual
and explanatory notes to the original versions should consult the issue
of *RCS* in question. In addition to quoting Sewtor-Lowden's note below
on the variant readings of the last line of the third poem, I wish to point
out the editorial mannerism of his comment, preempting Liddell &
Scott, that the word at the beginning (at the end in the translation) of the
second line, *choiros* (χοῖρος), literally "piggy," is Corinthian slang usage
for female genitals (see Aristophanes, *Wasps* 1353), especially a smoothly-
shaven one typical of *hetairas*, which latter word appears in the singular
in the first line and is translated by me as "pro." Similarly idiosyncratic
is his explanation of *keles* (κέλης) in the third line (lit. "race horse") as
"the common word for the sexual position of the woman on top and
astride the man" (see Aristophanes, *Lysistrata* 60), such information
being apparently deemed necessary for the reader to grasp the drift of
the editor's argument that *os nikeson* (ὡς νικήσων) later in the line refers
to the fact that that position was "the most expensive and, thus most

fruitful, one that a working woman had to offer." Of greater service and relevance is the note on the words that end the last line.]

Since the last phrase in the last line reads "πρᾶγμ᾽ ἐντελῶς ἀν[....] ον" in a Myrsinus archive papyrus roll found in Philadelphia (Darb-el-Gerza), the three words most likely to make sense in the context are ἀνθρώπινον, ἀνόητον, and ἀνόνητον, especially since the exact number of intervening missing letters is conjectural. The latter two words find some, though small, support from a badly damaged piece of papyrus, found by Grenfell and Hunt in the astonishing crocodile tombs at Tebtynis (Umm-el-Baragât) that possibly records this poem, in which the antepenultimate letter in the last somewhat indecipherable word could be read as a ν or a τ. The best case, common good sense aside, is made for ἀνθρώπινον in a papyprus fragment from some mummy cartonnage, discovered at Oxyrhynchus, in which a highly fragmented but evident version of this poem ends with the word "ἀνθ [....] ον," a dead giveaway, as it were. One cannot help being reminded of the famous two scraps of papyrus that utterly changed the meaning, as we all know, of lines 18–21 of Sappho's fragment 16.

CORRESPONDENCES

[I am grateful to Dr. Diana DiSantis, successor to Professor Emeritus Hugh Sydle, as Fylfot Professor and Department Chair of Classics at the State University of Illinois, Winnetka, who went to considerable trouble to retrieve the following letter—in which I first learned of Jonathan Barker—from what she described to me "as the massively chaotic correspondence file-pile" of *The Review of Classical Studies*. I thank her and SUIW for permission to publish it here.]

Professor Joseph Fisher, PhD
February 5, 1952
Director of the Division of Classical Studies
Editor, *The Review of Classical Studies*
State University of Illinois, Winnetka

My dear Fisher—
You ask me to tell you something about the role of the late Anastas Krebs of Munich in the three reconstructions of Ananius of Clitor lyrics I have proposed you publish in *RCS*. I only met the man once, I'm afraid, but I learned of his interesting, if rudimentary, work on our poet, which he did decades ago while still a young man, from a student of mine who worked with him in Germany only weeks before the heart attack, which, unfortunately, as we all know, proved fatal. I am certain that you, like all of us, are aware of Krebs' reputation as a leading authority on warfare in the ancient world, even if you have not, though many of us have, read his magisterial monograph on the famous between-the-walls-of-Corinth battle. Did you know I barely escaped the task of translating it when I was just starting out? Good old Graysie kept pressing me to do it as a way of getting my foot into the door of the profession with an early publication, but as luck would have it I resisted and, as we all know, went on to other things. In any event, Krebs, who may have sensed his end was nearing (as the Greeks nowadays say, saw there was little left of his bread), not only gave his work on Ananius to Jack Barker, my aforementioned student, who, by the by, will soon be hunting for a position, but also provided him with a complete narration of his passionate involvement with Ananius, his visits to Greece, which included inspections of the ruins

and what he called "the atmosphere" of Clitor, of his difficulties gaining acceptance of his work by his seniors, and some terrible events affecting him personally not far from Clitor during the last war. Barker was all too willing to relay this Greco-Teutonic saga to me in all of its gory details, but, as you all know, I am deeply engaged with my own work on the tragedians and thus asked him to spare me. As poor old Krebs surely intended the final destination of his Ananius material to be my hands, I took it off of Barker's, who was, I daresay, all too happy to be rid of it. If, as I suspect, Krebs showed it to his former mentor at Heidelberg, the great Armin Giesing, he likely received very little encouragement from that quarter for such an inchoate effort, there are just too many traces of the man Krebs throughout. But, as you know, my good friend and colleague, the three I sent you in my latest correspondence represent the first resurrections of K's desultory transcriptions that my assistant, Hugh Sydle, and I have been able to create out of material that is refractory enough, coming from various papyrological sources and fragments in the first place. I think you will agree we have imposed some order into the worlds "without form and void" of Ananius and Krebs by offering these little gems that would adorn a few pages of a future number of your excellent review. (I would not worry much over the obscenity issue concerning the third poem, for as I heard Graysie once say to Housman "the possibility of an undesirable, unsavoury outcome from the disclosure of a so-called obscenity is virtually nil when the beholding eye belongs exclusively to persons who read Latin and Greek as easily as they drink water.") Assuming this is agreeable, I will compose a brief introductory note for the three poems, in which I will, of course, give appropriate credit to AK, and have the resourceful Sydle send it to you as soon as I have completed work on the Euripides project. Until then, as you surely know, I remain

Yours faithfully,

MS-L

Kythe/Cambridge

P.S. How far is Winnetka from Toronto? I am doing a series of lectures there during March and April on Euripides and will have some time between commitments. It would be good to meet with you again, if possible, and talk about your visiting here some day in future. Have a jolly time.

[The following correspondence was filed among the papers belonging to the late Jonathan Barker that have been stored in four boxes in the archives of St. Thomas's School Harpenden, where Barker taught Greek and Latin for more than thirty years. I am grateful to Wink Barker, née Cavanaugh, the scholar's widow and school librarian, for responding to my inquiries concerning her husband's connection with the Ananios poems published in *RCS*, 31 with xerox copies of these letters. According to Mrs. Barker, at some point in time before she knew him well, her husband, who had saved these letters, arranged them in a series. Each sheet is preserved in a plastic sleeve, and the entire correspondence has been bound in a loose-leaf folder in descending chronological order. All items have been reproduced from original manuscript or typescript texts, Barker's surviving in carbon copy form, which Mrs. Barker claims her husband, a gifted typist, invariably made for everything he ever typed up. The temptation to reverse their hysteron-proteron order in this transcription was discouraged both by Mrs. Barker and the following verses typed on a label affixed to the front cover of the folder:

> hourglass hourglass
> your words of sand have run
> no longer are you hourglass
> when all your turns have done

Given the responsibilty of choosing between including or omitting this oddly organized gathering of communications as a part of the continuing reception of the poems of Ananios, I have decided to include it here in light of the small light it may shed on a subject whose history partakes of darkness enough. Though our glass—taking a hint from the verbal play in the little verse Barker either quoted (from?) or more likely composed himself—is one through which we see but darkly, we are still obliged to clarify what we can of the dim and obscure reflections it holds of us.

Dr. and Mrs. Barker had been colleagues for many years when they married just five years before Jonathan's death in 1984. Recently retired, Wink is now in the process of preparing her husband's Cambridge dissertation on the discourse of heroes for submission to scholarly presses.]

26 Jan. 1953
St. Thomas's School Harpenden

Sir Michael Sewtor-Lowden
Master, Kythe College
Cambridge University

Sir:

After all these months of silence on my part, I make this one exception in the name of ironic closure.

Received from you today a signed copy of *RCS* offprint of the three Ananius poems. Allow me to suggest an appropriate subtitle, "The Fleecing of Anastas Krebs!" I am stunned and astonished by what you have done *and* announce—an even greater, indeed a golden fleecing! I read enough of the Ananius work that Professor Krebs placed in my hands (for safekeeping, the poor man!) when I was in Munich to see that you have quite simply STOLEN IT. I cannot decide which is more hair-raising, your disingenuous and deliberately misleading introductory note, or the insincerity of your inscription to me: " For my dear Jack. Without whom, as we all know, these little poems would never have escaped oblivion." As we all know, indeed! Wouldn't a decent mentor have shared this minor publication with the student from whom he appropriated it? That is, if he had intended to use its matter honestly. Clearly, your perfidious plans—master of connivance that you are—could never include me, for I would surely have given you away—for dead preferably—(to echo one of your own deeply self-betraying locutions), and still may, if I can find the means and summon the fighting spirit your better in every way taught me. I would tan your hide, if I could, for your presumptuous taking of that which was never intended for you! My blood thins at the realization that your show of unhappiness and grief over AK's death was just that, a mere show from a position free of any immediate hazard that really masked, quite grotesquely, the opposite emotion, for which we English typically do not have a word, despite Burke's eloquent talking round it in his "Philosophical Inquiry," and must borrow one from the Germans. The hypocrisy!

So, you have handpicked Sydle—an excellent choice, whom you may just as well have begotten as taught. Did you know, according to him, your colleagues refer to you as the "Big Noise from Northampton"? To think that once I would have done anything in my power to keep that from you! But just to show you the editorial skills you have passed over—I think I would emend the word "Noise" to "Wind."

ΑΕΡΟΛΕΣΧΗΣ

You will blow right out of my book's dedication!

jb

#

1 April 1952

My dear Jack—

Please excuse the brevity of this note. I am in the Chicago area, lecturing and visiting with old friends. You should know that I have spoken warmly to Fisher about you. As you well know, I was not only taken by surprise with the news of K's passing but even more by my abiding grief over it. As my dear, departed German friend's favourite modern poet, whom he often quoted, wrote, "nur die Klage lernt noch." Which goes to show how deeply we may elegize ourselves through others. But I must let go of it and learn to subordinate Rilke to Euripides, whose Antigone advises, "our woeful tale wearies the gods." It will not be long before I can unequivocally announce that I have recovered my Gelassenheit. How poignant, that I should spontaneously use one of his favourite words here! One thing more, you will have learned by now that I asked Hugh Sydle to assist me with my Toronto lectures before my departure for North America. My only reason for not asking you was that I knew you were in a state of D. Phil. post partum depression, a common phenomenon, as we all know, and not exactly a frame of mind conducive to proof-reading text and vetting quotations. All this compounded, I divine, by your profound, though bravely undemonstrated, bereavement over K's unexpected demise. Let me reassure you there will be other times when I shall call upon you. In the meanwhile, hold on to the offer from St. Thomas's Harpenden, as even a temporary position makes one's candidacy more attractive than no position at all. Yours, M S-L.

[In the small space left at the bottom of this sheet, Jonathan Barker has written: "Must recover my own gelassenheit; wonder if poor, distracted

K ever regained his, such as it was, before he died? Can't say I recall his ever having used the word with me."]

#

February 29, 1952

Dear Hugh,

No wonder I haven't heard from you—you've moved up in the world, you clever Sheffield boy. You can imagine my surprise and delight when they told me at IBC that you had taken a job at WILLIAM GROSSMANN LTD and had moved to London in early November. We probably passed each other unwittingly on the way in and on the way out. I find it curious, though, that Sir Michael (about whom more below) didn't tell me this wonderful news, knowing we are old shipmates. Well, isn't that just like him. And he was running back and forth to London working on another script for the BBC, "Euripides, Innovator and Rebel" or something like that. An idea, he says, that came to him when he attended some performances at Epidaurus last summer. Anyway, my heartiest congratulations to you AND to myself, for having a friend in a high place—though as I do not yet know your title I cannot say how high your place within the high place is. You will let me know all of the details, of course. What with you there and me just completing the degree and headed for a faculty appointment somewhere, perhaps the States, we have come quite a way from the dreary old days when, thanks to the old man, we slaved away on the Greek course at JACT. Quite a leap forward, I'd say, and appropriately so in a Leap Year—in fact today's the day itself, mine own tetradic celebration, and a Friday to boot. Good omen. Sneeze loudly and check the flight of birds!

Speaking of signs, Hugh, I wanted to mention that several days ago as I was proofing my final deposit copy and listening in the background to Wagner on the wireless, I suddenly heard something, as if from εὐρύοπα Ζεύς. Unaware of the passing time and the change in programme, I suddenly found myself hearing a kind of between the teeth whistling, "zee zee, zee zee zoo zai zee zee / zee zai, zee zee zoo zee zai," (something like that). Then I'm certain I heard the host's voice say, "'The Big Noise from Winnetka.' And don't forget to credit Bobcat Bob Haggart for the lovely bass fiddle work and spiracular solo." (*Spiracular*, can you imagine? I swear it was the word he used!) That must have been the source of the notorious "Sewtor-Lowden Song" I thought to myself. That is it, is it not? I assume this little joke on our peerless leader alludes to the manner and not the substance of his discourse. Must admit that at our last few conferences he could not stop talking once he got started, as if his breath were escaping from the ox-hide wallet Aeolus gave Odysseus, so unchecked were his words. Or are his colleagues more malicious than we? The old boy must never know we're privy to this, I'm certain you agree, though I hope one day to be in a position to explain just how uncanny all of this is.

Congratulations again and write me—that's an order.

Cheers,

Jack

P. S. Out of idle curiosity, I tracked down Winnetka in the world atlas. One of many fascinating Indian names the country is filled with. A little north of Chicago on Lake Michigan and means "Beautiful Land" in Potawatomi. A far cry from Northampton, despite their shared amphibrachic cadence.

#

January 30, 1952

Dear Hugh,

I apologize for not getting in touch with you after I returned from Munich on November 2, but I had so much to do to finish my *Minacious*, and ("as we all know") keeping up with himself was almost impossible. But there it is, done, and I am Dr. Barker, Dr. Sydle, and pleased to meet you. And would be pleased to meet you in person for supper at the Greeks' on Trumpington Street and then on to The Eagle so we can wish ourselves a proper New Year. I want also to tell you all about the extraordinary and, alas, recently deceased Herr Doktor Professor Anastas Krebs, who gave me something in a few days that Sewtor-Lowden did not in years. He actually spoke of my work as publishable, going so far as to advise me to use something from the magnificent tympanum figures from the Temple of Aphaia that the Germans rescued from certain oblivion for my cover design or a frontispiece. But I mustn't make further complaint, for the old boy saw me through the final stages, just as you said he would. And he has promised to place me in an American university, to boot. I cannot believe he is anything but utterly sincere in this, though I am a bit more unnerved rather than amused, I must confess, by the story you told me just before I left for Germany about how some members of the department have dubbed him " The Big Noise from Northampton" after an American jazz number about a place called Winnebago, or something like that.

As I am still phoneless, as I am sure you are as well, I will ring you at work in the Biographical Centre from a public phone so we can get together and a lift a glass or two to ourselves and to our esteemed Mentor

Cheers,

Jack

#

Hôtel Lutétia
43 Blvd. Raspail
Paris 6^e
6 January 1952

Dear Jack,

Anastas Krebs is dead, dear boy—struck down by Zeus' bright thunderbolt! Apparently of a heart attack in Greece on December 13, while hiking, or just after, up the wooded mountain slopes near Kalavryta. This I learned in a letter, sent on to me here in Paris by my housekeeper, from the son of the eminent Armin Giesing, Wilhelm, a scholar who, as we all know, has made something of a name for himself with a rather free-wheeling meditative study about the influence of ancient thought on Goethe. The very man, I am sure, with whom you reported Krebs as having had an unpleasant exchange outside his office in one of your letters to me. The two of them shared some ugly history, I believe, in the early thirties when Giesing was teaching at Freiburg and Krebs had protested the treatment of some of the faculty there to its rector. Giesing's letter was brief and to the point, written, he announced, as an academic courtesy since what turned out to be K's ultimate professorial activity involved one of my students, an honour, he remarked, that K could not resist reminding his colleagues of almost daily. He said that K had suffered several heart attacks in recent years and that nobody, including himself, expected he had long to live. Nothing from the German end, however, to shed light on Krebs' precipitous decision to go to Greece, but Giesing did reveal, to my great surprise and bewilderment, that he had tried to have poor old Krebs buried there at his own expense, but the Greek government insisted on returning K's remains and his personal effects to Munich. To the revelation of this rather private matter, he added the odd bit of information that he had discovered what a colleague who had served in the military confirmed were two spent machine-gun shells in the bottom of K's briefcase beneath a mess of crumpled sheets and scraps of paper. Though I concede one would have no way of knowing how long they were in there, I find this picture unusually disconcerting, yet I cannot say why. I can imagine someone like Gieising wanting to degrade any sympathy one might feel for our poor, departed Anastas ("may his memory be eternal," as the Greek Orthodox requiem intones) by emphasizing his eccentricity to the end. But enough about what cannot be remedied. You and I, however, are in positions to reciprocate K's kind and generous good offices. First, I must attempt to place some of his Ananius reconstructions in *RCS*, whose editor, John Fisher, is an old friend, the very man to whom I have been planning to write in your behalf. How providential that K had given you his early work on lyric poetry to give to me, for it is high time he gained some recognition for it, albeit posthumously. I am committed to doing something useful with this material. Of course, as we all know, K's most original work was *Der korinthischer Krieg: Versuch einer Neubewertung*, in which he audaciously challenges Xenophon's account in the *Hellenica*, allegedly based on the tales of eyewitnesses, of the slaughter by the Spartans of the Corinthian democrats' Argive allies who were trapped between the two long city walls with their backs to the stockade. This daring and stirring work of scholarship still remains untranslated into English, though I have heard there are inferior versions of it in Italian and Modern Greek. Think, dear boy, of devoting a few months to putting this book into English, an ideal activity after the dissertation rigors, by the way. A finely conceived and well-made book, as we all know, may endure longer than a luckless child. Do it quickly for poor Krebs, for the enduring memory of his name and to launch the notice of your own. Our legacy is all. I shall never forget the pathos of the recently departed L. Wittgenstein's remark at one of his rare appearances at a faculty gathering a few years ago, when out of that unshakeably stern face came the words, "The only seed I am likely to sow is a jargon."

As you know, I came here immediately after the New Year to confer with Professor Folliet about Racine et Euripide before I compose my next lecture for the BBC. You and I had had a rather hasty meeting ourselves before I left and I wanted to clarify the intentions behind some of my parting remarks about the change in the character of your prose in places from the usual scholarly genteel to the aggressive, indeed, almost bellicose. They were merely descriptive, not to be taken as a coded message suggesting further revision. This post-Krebsian development, if that is what it in fact is, is not an altogether unhappy result of your topic's taking control over you at crucial moments in your discourse, dear boy. This, as we all know, can and does happen to the best of us and serves to liven up the humdrumtidum of the life academic. Your text is fine, just check it for typos and bibliographical errors, and have it ready for me when I return to Cambridge later this month.

As for our friend K, that gifted, gloriously trained scholar who appears to have succumbed to severe distraction and a broken heart, do not grieve overmuch for him, but leave that to me. "Dans le fond de mon coeur vous ne pouviez pas lire." [Racine, *Phèdre* II. v. 598]

Yours,
        M S-L

P. S. Now that he is gone, I shall treasure all the more your vivid descriptions of what were to be that singular man's last days.

[At the bottom of the last page of this letter, the following sentences appear in Barker's longhand: "Did K really intend for me to turn over his work on Ananius to S-L? Or did he mean for *me* to take it on? Now that I have at last looked up the rest of the sentence quoted from X on the back of K's card, I must ponder that seriously. Though maybe I was supposed to play the messenger, a kind of Hermes? But Hermes would not have allowed the goods to be plucked right out of his hand. *Au contraire.* Hermes manqué then? One thing of which I am certain, I will not translate that monograph on the Corinthian business, though I will not declare this decision very soon. But the dedication to 'Minacious Discourse', when it's published, may very well read:

> For Sir Michael Sewtor-Lowden
> And in Memory of Anastas Krebs

Find, perhaps, a fitting quotation with which to head it."]

#

Kythe College   11 October 1951
Cambridge

My dear boy, Jack,

So it's true, Krebs does conduct saltatory interviews. I had heard this rumor more than once, which you unfortunately bore the burden of confirming, but had quite forgotten about it. Please forgive me for not remembering that and for failing to warn you that he can be somewhat eccentric, as so many of us know. First and foremost, it appears he has given you useful bibliographic information and some constructive criticism about your delivery (no need for me to review this as long as it does not change the essential argument). K—as you call him—always knew how to land his blows in a scholarly controversy. So take these good things and forget all those other aberrant behaviours and allegations you have so graphically conveyed to me. He always had a strong daemonic side but it seems to have gone terribly awry. Still, this is a Proteus worth the mastering—"γέρων ἅλιος νημερτής"—if one knows what to seek from him. By all means, do continue your München sojourn as planned, do your reading, and find out, as best you can, about that other work he was engaged in during his relentless researches into warfare. I will be very surprised if it hasn't to do with a minor poet he once mentioned to me named Ananius of Clitor, a later poet than the minor-minor one of the same name who is well-known for his "broken-hipped" lines. Coraggio, dear boy, soon you will be back in Cambridge, well before the end of Michaelmas, and on your way. Speaking of which, you'll be pleased to learn Hugh Sydle has just now completed his work for the degree, and a great pleasure to work with him it was, though he cannot compete with you when it comes to command of Greek, critical percipience and sensitivity to language. I always thought the two of you would more or less finish the race together.

Finally, do not be overly concerned with our German freund and his idiosyncratic displays. After all, the absence of any substantive reservation in his critique of your manuscript clearly indicates the quality of work that we have accomplished here. Though his odd, but really unmalicious, conduct may have unnerved you a bit, you must keep in mind that his imprimatur is invaluable. If I say to you humour him, indulge him, I am confident you will be capable of doing it without patronizing him. We certainly do not want to turn him against us. So do keep writing your vivid accounts of your encounters with him, which I do enjoy so, and listen for all he reveals about himself and his work.

Looking forward to your next, I remain,

Truly yours,

M S-L

P.S. It occurs to me I ought to warn you that the price for this may be having to subject yourself to unendurably long recitations of German poetry, as I did once upon a time myself when, both of us a bit tipsy, Krebs recited for me Goethe's—I was later to learn famous vampire—poem "Die Braut von Korinth," a work he was forced to commit to memory at the age of four and which he claimed left its indelible marks upon the progress of his personal and professional lives. Fortunately, I was fortified against the lugubrious and lurid effects of both the poem and its performance by a generous pitcher of deliciously chilled Corinthian restina and I strongly urge you to take similar spirituous refuge should the occasion arise.

#

Professor Doktor Anastas Krebs
September 17, 1951
Department of Classical Studies
Ludwig-Maximilians Universität

My dear Krebsie—
You are certainly entitled to be astonished, as you may well be, to hear from me after so many years, our last correspondence, as we both know, having occurred well before the outbreak of the war. The immediate cause of my writing is to present to you the bearer of this letter, my student Jonathan Barker, who is trying to do something useful with the battle speeches in the *Iliad*. He is near the completion of his dissertation, which he insists on calling "Minacious Discourse," and could use some constructive criticism from an old Schlachtross like you. Would you be so good as to read over what Jack has written and lend him a helping hand? He is a somewhat obsessive but unassertive young man who compensates for his lack of brilliance with a strong dose of diligence. Though he is not, as our Irish friends say, the sharpest knife in the drawer full of my current students, I assure you he will respond with meticulous obedience to your suggestions, being one of those decently frail spirits in need of a father. I hope you do not object to this request, but when I inquired at the university concerning your whereabouts and learned you were to be back in Munich this autumn I became excited at the prospect of my student benefiting from your deep and wise understanding of the subject. So I place him and his work in your good hands and hope you will forgive me for sending him to you unannounced —frankly, I did not want to risk a rejection on personal terms, which I would understand though it would assuredly wound me. But the nightmare is over. I know you will not turn him away from your door once he is there. *Urbanus et instructus semper.* As we both know, you always enjoyed a good surprise and a jolly time.

I suppose my writing is a dead giveaway—I am eager to renew our old friendship and will write you again after Jack returns to Cambridge.

Yours of old,

M S-L

[At the bottom of this letter, Barker has written an explanation of how it came into his possession. "In the summer of 1962, as I was gathering whatever documents I had in which signs of my betrayal lurked, I looked once again at the dissertation draught that I had taken with me to Germany. Amidst the bibliography pages I found this traitorous letter of introduction and two unrelated photos (?), left there inadvertently, it would seem (but who's to know?) by Krebs after he had read the text and returned it to me. Thus, after believing I had come to the end of my decade-long realization of Sewtor-Lowden's treachery, I discovered I had not known its murky wellspring, which is here." A new paragraph follows in which Barker refers briefly to the two black and white souvenir photographs, undated and without postmark, which had probably been originally mailed to Krebs as enclosures: the first, of eight young German soldiers posing in front of the Parthenon, the second, of six soldiers standing beside a rock face with flowing water. Mrs. Barker kindly xeroxed these two photos front and back (a bit on the dark side and on ordinary paper) and enclosed them in her packet to me. Written on the back of the first is the message, "Die schönste Zeit." with "Dein Neffe S" just below. On the back of the second, in the same hand are the words, "Der ΑΛΥΣΣΟΣ : Es war Phantastisch!" Barker writes of these, "I have no clear explanation for the presence of these photos among these papers. I am certain, however, that S is K's nephew Siegfried, and that, though it is hard to say for sure which of these eight and six is Siegfried, the one who stands second to the left in the first and the one cupping his hands as if to catch the water in the second bear a fairly strong resemblance. Is this accidental or is it K's way of communicating to me something about how important our meeting had been for him, or his expectations of me?"]

#

[A last undated sheet in this group of documents contains the following curiously titled "JB's Final Verses," whose contents indicate composition with a *terminus a quo* of 1975, owing to the death in that year of Sir Michael Sewtor-Lowden. The first of these verses, with its reference to Dionisius Petavius, or Denis Petau, who in 1627 proposed that we term dates before AD as BC but failed to insert a 0 year between 1 BC and 1 AD, not only hints at a reason for Barker's self-ironizing remarks, perhaps, but also for the exclusion of this page from the descending chronological order that connects the preceding letters.]

> The absence 'tween B. C. and A. D. of zero
> Should not mean J. Barker cannot be its hero.
> It's befitting that he, with Petavian key,
> Was locked in the cell that confined his career-0.

•

> The Sewtor-Lowden Song
> > *allegretto con brio*

> Big noise came in from Winnetka,
> Big noise went right out again.

> Big noise came in from Northampton,
> Big wind failed to be humane.

> Big noise fell right through fenêtre,
> Big wind won't be heard again.

•

> First Ananius invented ischiorrhogics,
> Second of Clitor awaited his scholar Krebs,
> Whose words 'Big Noise' thieved from me with lying lips.
> But now at last Nemesis comes—black rogue broke hips!

•

What was covered
Will be uncovered.
Well, let it be me,
Oh, Mummy,
Let it be by me.

*

Beautiful Land,
What were you to me?
An onomatopotawatami.

*

[The following letters from Munich, all of them written in longhand, by Jonathan Barker to Sir Michael Sewtor-Lowden concerning his consultations with Anastas Krebs, are printed here with the kind permission of the firm of Burke, Potter & Quimby, Solicitors, trustees of the Sewtor-Lowden Estate. Due to the circumstances of Barker's time in Munich, especially the fact that he did not take a portable typewriter with him, these are most likely the only extant versions of the letters that he wrote from that city; if he had composed first drafts and kept them, they probably would have been found by Mrs. Barker among his archival materials.]

Munich, 25 September, 1951

Dear Mentor,

Thanks to your inspired idea that I come to Munich and your good offices in my behalf with the AAC in securing my BEA airfare and Spartan per diem expenses, I have arrived, found myself a comfortable accommodation here at the Pensione Gabriele, Schönfeldstrasse in the Schwabing district, just a few steps from the University. And yesterday, I took those steps directly and presented myself with your letter of introduction to "Herr Doktor Professor Anastas Krebs." I was not quite prepared for the enthusiasm with which he received me—simply on the basis of my spoken explanation of my presence. After our mutual discovery that his conversational English is considerably better than my German—I don't recall your informing me his English was so excellent, though his accent becomes stronger as he becomes more animated—we agreed to conduct our business in English, the first of which was for me to leave my chapters with him and to return at three on Friday, the 28th. He did not open your letter in my presence, saying he preferred to read the chapters before he saw what you had to say about them and me. As I left, he assured me—I hope you will not think me a rude fellow if I approximate his charming accent—that "Vee vill haf cholly time," and handed me his card, on the back of which this is printed:

ἄρχοντος γάρ ἐστιν οὐχ ἑαυτον μόνον ἀγαθὸν παρέχειν.
—*Cyropaedia*, II. i. 11

A guiding principle of his, or something like that, I imagined as I read it but was not confident enough to question him about it.

I thought of waiting until after my meeting with him on Friday to write you a full account, which I fully intend to do, but I must write you today to convey my gratitude for your sending me on this adventure. I feel like Telemachus, setting sail over the wine dark sea in search of tidings.

Your sincerely grateful student,

Jack

#

October 4, 1951

Dear Professor Sewtor-Lowden,

Having met twice with Professor Krebs, on the 28th of September and yesterday, since I first wrote you from this place, I find myself in the odd position of being compelled to report to you at greater length about the behaviour of K than about his reactions to my dissertation. Just so that you will not suffer misgivings about having directed me to him, I can assure you that his close, thorough reading has been helpful, but, aside from a number of valuable bibliographical suggestions, is almost exclusively addressed to the style and tone of my manner of arguing my points. I will spend time looking up and reading the references he gave me in the library here (he has generously written me a letter requesting permission to use the collections) and making sense of his marginal commentaries about revisions. Since I did not bring a typewriter with me, serious revising will have to wait until I return to England, as will the opportunity for you to read his singular comments for yourself, if you care or have the time to.

As for Prof. K's conduct at our two meetings, it was very strange, as I am certain you will agree once you have read this, yet not unrelated, in his mind I think, to his general response to my writing. But to get to my unusual narrative: as soon as he saw me at his office door, he leapt out of his chair and rushed across the room to an old phonograph player, which he wound up energetically and then played a recording of the famous "Pilgrim Chorus" from Wagner's *Tannhäuser*. With outspread arms, he invited me to dance to the music, which he referred to as the hero's music of the soul, or something like that. He exhorted me to join him, "Tanz, tvirl, svay, do not be afraid, you may rise to your death wiz honor, Todt mit Ehre, to such music!" Need I say how terribly embarrassed I was by this reception? Self-consciously, I joined him, stepping gingerly and smiling like an idiot, I'm afraid, at his reddened, entranced face. Then, to my great relief, he turned the bloody thing off, muttering to himself, "Er hat aber kein Rhythmus!" (I have enough of an ear for German to understand that!) Sitting down finally, K stared at me for a good moment as he labored to catch his breath and then began to preach to me about my ambitions to write about the way the heroic "warriurss" address each other. He told me I must learn to express the rhythms of such discourse through my body, not just my mind, with all my being. Then suddenly as all this began, it came to an end. He handed me my chapters, told me to study his comments carefully, and to return on the third of next month, when we would do this again.

Because of this last remark, I decided to wait until after that conference to write you, that is, after I found out if "doing this again" referred simply to our meeting or to tripping 'the fright fantastic' with him around his office. Neither possibility does justice to what occurred.

Yesterday, as I arrived punctually at Krebs' office the music was already playing, only this time it was Greek folk music. Left hand raised above his head, he offered me his handkerchief. "Tsámiko, circle tanz of ze warriurss!" I took it as he simultaneously pulled me along and used me as a support. "Toum tiri toumti toumti toum, tiri toumti toumti toum," he intoned synchronically with the recording, stomping and kicking his feet in a pattern of tiny, yet vigorous, athletic steps. He was rather remarkable for a stout little bald man surely well into his sixties. Two of his colleagues passing outside his door quickly looked in and then snapped their heads away as if in disgust. A common occurrence? I wondered. Oblivious, K danced on, snapping fingers of his extended right hand and almost pulling me to the floor with a combination squat-twirl-squat that ended with a leap, right leg kicked back which he slapped on the outside heel. "OHPA! Now you say it. Say OHPA!" He laughed and shook his head at my feeble antiphony.

Still standing, after a brief pause to recapture his breath, he solemnly recited in perfect English the title of my dissertation: "Minacious Discourse: Warrior Speech in Homer's *Iliad*." Another moment of silence, and then beginning, "My dear Chack," he erupted into a stream of agitated exclamations as he stalked around the room about how Thucydides was right about the poets not providing the best evidence about the conduct of war. But the poets, he insisted we must allow, have always held the key to the emotions of warriors, just as they do to those of lovers, to all the secrets of men and women, as Walter (?) sings. Whether or not they have been to war or been great lovers themselves, the poets have the power to understand these states and their friction upon the soul, a subject he has not altogether ignored during his career, he said. Still his lifelong study of mankind's most abiding and appropriate monument, Kriegführung, warfare, the craft that never fails, never ends, has delivered to him the greatest appreciation of its dazzling strategic and technological feats in antiquity. You will want to know, Sir Michael, that at this point he said that was why he refused, at that time (to what time does he refer?), your offer to translate his book on the war in Corinth, for he had already lost interest in it, having been inspired to undertake a searching comparative analysis of Thucydides and one Clausewitz (not, I infer, a classicist but some kind of military scholar), a daring and original project! Even though this Clausewitz (I must look him up), he said, correctly claimed that in all the military history of modern Europe there is no example of a Marathon, there is no reason why modern scholarship should not strive to remove some of the impediments to a cultural agreement between us and the ancients on something so fundamentally human as conducting ourselves in battle just as strenuously as it struggles to overcome the historical diversities of our conduct in love. He had hoped to sort out and neutralize the disorienting swerves and shifts in the history of human consciousness, as contended in the great poet's (?) lines that when new creeds arise love and truth are uprooted like foul weeds, but, alas, he failed to dismantle the walls time builds around the past and he abandoned this work, but not without hope that his successors may one day succeed where he did not. And, besides, he had also about this same time begun his unfinished work on a minor, but to him very important, amatory poet. He imagined himself, he laughed, a Hephaestus figure struggling to capture the truth about Aphrodite and Ares in the nets of his scholarship. But he had lost the one in whom he had placed his hopes of carrying on his work, but now just as he believed it was too late for any cure for the mad dog's bite . . . He did not complete this thought, but began another, about why there could be no lion monument at his sister son's grave, which I found impossible to follow, as he was moving in vehement circles around the room. Then finally, he picked up and unsheathed an army dagger from his desk and held it up to my face for me to see the skull and crossbones on its pommel and the legend "Meine Ehre Heisst Treue" embossed on its blade. "Let there be honour!" he cried, "let us swear by the relentless waters of Styx!"

Needless to say, I was quite taken aback by this performance and needed a moment's respite from it as much as K did as he finally sat down. His demeanour now completely changed to one of gaiety, he admonished me to dance no more with mincing steps, nor to mince my words about the minacious --to learn to "hop light" on my feet. Beside himself with pleasure, he took my hand in both of his and reveled in his wordplay: "Hah! I make a paranomasia. Wortspiel—called in English? Yes, a pun! Hold your pen, Chack, as if it is your spear." Strong writing can kill, he went on, a recitation or a piece of paper with just a few words on it can kill! Look at Archilochos, that warrior poet, and Hipponax, his sometime fellow fighter in limping iambics, they both made deadly weapons of their poems. He then told me to go back to work and to come back to see him soon, but not until after I had gone to hear a performance of *Daphne* by Strauss at the Staatsoper and to look at the Rubens in Der Alte Pinakotek and the pedimental sculptures of "the beautiful warriurss" fighting at Troy in the Der Alte Glyptothek.

I hope you will not think the less of me if I confess that I am utterly perplexed and ready to depart for home at the earliest opportunity. Would you be so kind as to give me your impressions of this and some guidance. I anxiously await your letter. In the meantime, I shall go to the museums, as I was planning to take some time for them anyway, but not to *Daphne*, the price of admission to that being quite beyond my means.

Yours anxiously but sincerely,

Jack

P.S. I almost forgot to mention that all of this was topped off with an altercation between Krebs and one of the two colleagues who had passed by his office during the Greek folk dance. As K was seeing me out of his office, this professor, a thin grey little man, emerged from his directly across the hall and looked coldly at us but said nothing. K stopped and, gesturing in my direction, announced me in German to the man. I made out my name, your name, and Cambridge University in what sounded like a formal introduction. The man stood there, acknowledging me with the slightest nod of his head but persisted in not speaking to K, who then gestured in his direction and said to me, "Wilhelm Giesing, one of the pride of Freiburg." Then to my astonishment, he recited this couplet:

> And lo! her bird, (a monster of a fowl,
> Something betwixt a Heidegger and owl,)

This Giesing then began a low, hissing tirade that got louder and louder at K, who giggled and whispered "Pope's 'Dunciad'" in my ear as he whisked me away quickly to the stairwell and down the stairs. I can't help but feel this was a stirring up of an old stew, perhaps something to do with the war years, though I have no idea what role K may have played, if he had one at all.

#

Thursday
October 18, 1951

Dear Professor Sewtor-Lowden,

The anticipation with which I await your response to my last letter has lost some of its nervous edge by virtue of my fortuitous meeting with Professor Krebs on the street this morning. Though I still look forward to your words of guidance, I thought I should not delay communicating to you the marked alteration, if not the total easing, of the mental torment he had previously caused in me by what occurred this morning in his office.

As I said, we ran into each other on the street and he insisted I accompany him to his office. Once there, he made directly for the victrola and played a recording from Wagner again, from *The Flying Dutchman*, I think. To my surprise, I began to dance before he had a chance to ask me, and with notable abandon, which seemed to please him greatly. I even removed my fountain pen from my jacket and held it up and out beside my right ear as if it were some kind of weapon. Eyes narrowed, he scrambled to his desk and seized the German officer's dagger, then with a chuckle put it down and picked up a sharply pointed pencil in its stead. He grabbed a volume of Pauly-Wissowa out of a bookcase and motioned for me to do the same. "Pick up your hoplon, hoplite, and fight, fight, fight!" We held them in our left hands like shields. And thus we mock-duelled and danced through the duration of the recording. Do not ask me to account for this initiative; all I can say is my inspiration for it seemed quite spontaneous.

K then asked me what I thought of the Glyptothek and if I had seen the Rubens (no mention of the opera) and began immediately to talk about his numerous paintings depicting the Last Judgment. I recalled the torrential showers of plump, pink bodies falling every which way into the infernal depths countered by another rosy column of chubby bodies that seemed to float or to be climbing an invisible ladder heavenwards. "Ja! Es ist wie ein Fleischmarkt," he replied, "like ze meat store," as his mother had told him when he was a little boy. Then he recited a rhyming couplet in German, which he told me came from the "Walpurgisnacht" of Goethe's *Faust*, a proverbial but eloquent condemnation of the folly of the masses, "die Menge," about how truth and beauty are wasted on them, like Hamlet's "caviare to the general." And as for Rubens' representations of the ancients, both mortal and immortal, they were a disgrace: "nothing but pink meat und fat!" An allegorisation of his soft-headed views on war, whose antithesis could be read in the magnificent warrior sculptures in the Glyptothek. Then strolling around his office, he quietly explained that Rubens was the kind of art that should have been condemned by the Third Reich as "Entartete Kunst," a position that nobody really understood and could have got him into a lot of trouble had he persisted in advocating it in public. As it was, the intervention of a relative in a high place was crucial, warding off an official rebuke, or worse, and the same relative warned him to keep his professorial eccentricities to himself, which, he admitted, he had done—to his great shame. But he was pleased to see I agreed with him about the degeneracy of Rubens! (I thought it best not to contest this point). It had taken him a longer time, he said, to convince his nephew Siegfried, whom he was personally training as a scholar. This Siegfried, he seemed to be confessing, needed toughening up, "too much Ganymede and not enough Ilus, you see." His voice choked with emotion, he held up both index fingers, as if to signify a quotation, and said the only lubricant against such an abrasion is combat, something like that. Words could not express (a doubtful allegation) his pleasure, he went on, at today's indications that I was becoming a scholar warrior and was beginning to embrace the heroic ethos body and soul. He wanted me to fight for my positions and was glad to see I was giving every sign of being prepared to do so, to take for my model as a scholar the Homeric Odysseus for whom the suitors, whose arms, turned to flab by their misuse, broke down miserably and were no match for him in the test of the bow. He was confident, he went on, that I would pass the tests in store for me, though I should always keep in mind that the world of scholarship is a battlefield to be won or lost by the most daring stratagem.

I would not argue with you if you pronounced all this utter foolishness and "unadulterated cattle-cakes." Do you recall the phrase? You once used it to characterize the outlandish translations of the Greek dramatists by the American Palmer D. Slavowitz in one of your unforgettable lectures. Yet I was deeply touched by K's care for me and my work that came through it. That, I am sure, explains my buoyant spirits, along with the realization that I shall soon be returning to England, the good Dr. K having informed me that our work together has been completed and that we will celebrate it a week from yesterday evening, when he intends to pass something of great importance to him into my hands.

Awaiting your kind letter, I remain

Yours truly,

Jonathan Barker

#

Friday, 4 AM
26 October 1951

Dear M S-L:

As you can see from the hour of my writing, I have been burning the midnight oil poring over the contents of a large packet which K gave me at our farewell dinner last night—no, night before last rather, the 24th. As you guessed, quite correctly, in your letter of October 11, which arrived the day after I posted my last letter to you, K's secret work does involve the poet Ananius of Clitor—in the form of work sheets and papers, including photocopies of what appear to be scholia and commentaries in Greek, towards an edition of his extant poems, which is to say, hand-printed copies and typescripts of transcriptions of A's poems and fragments covered with interlinear and marginal corrections, queries, comments, variants, etc. in pencil and ink. There is even a small fragment of papyrus, carefully wrapped in cellophane, which I took a stab at deciphering, but all I could make out so far were two phrases, " the lyre of Hermes" and "similarly sweet," I think, something like that. Fortunately, I recall seeing a transcription of it that Professor Krebs had already made among this abundance of learned particles and pieces. This packet he solemnly placed in my hands the other night in the Bahnhof, and willy-nilly I shall be carrying it, snuggled next to "Minacious Discourse" in my capacious briefcase when I return exactly a week from today on the 2nd of the coming month to England and into your able custody. Am I being happily, sappily proleptic? Or even using the term correctly? At this point I cannot care, and I think you will understand why.

When I went to meet K at his office in the late afternoon of the 24th, he invited me to go with him to his "favorite vatering hole," namely, the beer garden in the main Bahnhof. As we departed, he picked up an old leather pouch from his desk and raising it in front of me told me it contained a work-in-progress he wished to pass into my hands. Whether or not I succeeded in disguising the alarm this statement caused in me became moot, for as we moved into the hall he continued to chatter, stopping in front of the closed door of his antagonistic colleague's office. On the door's window was taped a narrow slip of paper with the words "Was muß geschehn, mags gleich geschehn!" elegantly hand printed on it. K pointed at it and with a burst of ironic laughter told me this was the first time it had made any sense to him personally.

During the cab ride, for which I insisted on paying, K embarked upon a rambling excursion on his own early days as a scholar, when as a precocious student in his early 20s he had traveled to Oxford to do research on the Corinthian War and took a side trip to Cambridge— some years before my mentor, meaning you, arrived there—and met an excitable young Austrian who was studying philosophy with Bertrand Russell. This Austrian, by whom he can only have meant our late Professor Wittgenstein, entertained young K and others one afternoon with a performance of amazing virtuosity in which he whistled the melodies of 'Die Forelle' and several other of Schubert's songs to the piano accompaniment of a young English friend. When I informed him that this young Austrian returned later to become a professor of philosophy and had passed away in April, he stared sadly out the window at the blur of yellow lights in the darkening city for a moment and said something to the effect that young men, delighted by all the idiotic things they are allowed to say and do, often see great futures in store for them. He eyed me as if about to say something important, but just then the cab arrived at our destination and he scrambled out the door clutching his leather bag to his chest.

Clearly, they know him at the Bahnhof, for we were promptly led to one of the few small tables in the enormous hall resonant with the sounds of hundreds of conversations and orders given and taken in German. Curiously, the ebullient human buzz in German public rooms sounds no different than that in places where English is spoken. Not so odd, actually, when you think about it. I cannot say how much beer and food in the form of platters of all kinds of wursts, potatoes, breads and krauts we consumed through the evening. Throughout the meal, he spoke animatedly about Ananius of Clitor and how he had become interested in his poems when he was a young scholar, now and then pausing to recite a fragment, making pronounced stops to indicate the lacunae. He told me how he had first interrupted his research on the Corinthian wars to reconstruct some of Ananius' poems and how he contrived to devote some of his time to work on them sub rosa throughout the years that he was building his reputation in the field of warfare in the classical world. Even the extensive travel to Greece that this work required of him gave him the chance to take more than one side trip to the Peloponnese in pursuit of the world of Ananius. He wanted to visit Clitor, to experience first hand "das Ambiente," its atmosphere. Then he drummed his fingers on the table two or three times before he continued. But like Goethe, going back in the footsteps of the "Triumvirn," in Roma, what he found there was something much more important than mere ruins, though ruins there were, which, though not extraordinary, were enough for him. Some big walls, a few towers, and the remains of a theatre in the fork between "two rifers." He found but a trace of the sanctuary that had once held bronze statues of the Dioscouri just outside the city according to Pausanias, he complained, but there were some fragments of Doric columns in the rubble of fallen churches. He went on and on, correcting Pausanias on his matching of rivers with phenomena, explaining that P mistakenly thought one of them was the Aroanios, where he waited in vain to hear the legendary fish singing. But Ananius, he explained, wrote of chirping fish in the river Ladon not very far away. Yes, what he found—or found him—there would be with him forever, was "mein irrefocable good luck—Glück," he insisted with great ardour, "Ein Mal, ein Mal, something or other." Then with a faraway look, he muttered, "Mutter, mutter," followed by some words unintelligible to me, ending with the phrase "die schöne Nacht".

From his earlier remarks I thought I had some idea where all this was going, but after every pause to raise his stein to his lips a new story poured out. He kept on talking about Clitor and how he had ridden a mule from there to the town of Kalavryta, near the monastery of Ayia Lavra where the Greek War of Independence began in 1821 when Archbishop Germanos administered the oath of revolt to the warriors. In antiquity Kalavryta (means "beautiful springs," he said, as if I couldn't have figured that out) had been a place called Kynaitha, home to a lawless and savage people—"the Worst of the Arcadians," he called them—who, he then informed me, had dedicated at Olympia a statue of Zeus with a thunderbolt in each hand. "Ze Aetolians vipe zem out in ze year 220, and ve try to do it again." Had it not been for the amount of beer I had ingested, this last statement, and what followed, would have registered with greater shock, but I numbly concentrated on his desultory narrative, which he was delivering with increasing intensity, for as it was not poetry but life he was reciting I could not successfully fortify myself against its effects, as you advised in your recent letter. It appears his nephew Siegfried, his only sister's only son, was part of the occupation force at Kalavryta during the war, an assignment K claimed to have arranged through his special family contact in Berlin, a first cousin, one General Hans Krebs. Cousin Hans, according to him, had handled the surrender negotiations with the Russians the week after Der Führer and Eva Braun had committed suicide and then dutifully took his own life. I tried to indicate to K that these were matters I did not care to know about, but there was no stopping him. Siegfried, whom he loved like a son and had groomed to be his successor, it happened, was one of some 81 German soldiers captured by the Greek communist resistance late in 1943 and lined up on the edge of a precipice on Mount Chelmos, near the source of the river Styx, and executed. When the German search party discovered the broken bodies of this "new Sacred Band" in the ravine below, the Kommandant, who had a younger brother in the doomed patrol, gave the order for all of the males over the age of 15 in Kalavryta to be collected and mowed down by machine gun fire as an atonement action. This so-called martyrdom, he argued, was essentially Greek in nature, a pure act of military revenge provoked by the communist guerillas, who later caused a civil war that far exceeded the German occupation in brutality. What happened was not much different from the Athenians putting to death all of the Melian men of military age after crushing them for their refusal to join the empire. But one must pay a high price for his hope, as Thucydides says, and besides, he went on, if he had remembered what Clausewitz (him again!) had said about the extreme dangers of Volkskrieg in mountainous countries perhaps Siegfried would still be alive today. "Mein Gram—grieff," he started to say but stopped when I threw up both of my hands, palms outward, at him. This abrupt action, along with the stares from people at neighboring tables quieted him at last.

After a long drink, he returned to the tale about his mule ride through the heart of Arcadia, and how he had stopped at the ruins of the Sanctuary of Artemis at Lusi on the road from Clitor to Kalavryta. "Austrians make a very good dig here, you know." The people of Clitor, he lectured, call her Artemis Hemerasia because Melampus brought the daughters of Proetus, who were mooing all over the Aroanios mountains, here, "nicht Sicyon," to cleanse them of their "mad-cow disease" with her sacred spring water. Ananius, he informed me, had started to write a poem about that clever old "blackfeeted" Melampus—then, correcting himself with a giggle, explained he did write such a poem but we have no more of it to read than its first line. The poet, he said, favoured Aphrodite over Artemis, being, as you call it, "ladies' man," who supposedly traveled often to Corinth to visit the Temple of Aphrodite, not the small sacred one on the Acrocorinithus, he qualified, but to the one down in the city, where hundreds of sacred prostitutes were available, as Pindar and others have shown. He himself had had some amorous adventures in these places, he confessed, turning a deeper shade of red than that already induced by the beer and energetic narration. As a devoted scholar, he had tried to follow his poet, to partake of what he gave him, he said nodding his head slowly. Then, though rather drunk, with his eyes closed made this remarkable quotation, "not vear ze carpet but valk zat vay he valked." My God, first Pope and now Yeats! After this, nothing about him would surprise me. How right you were to write about his being "a Proteus worth the mastering." Yet I cannot believe I have even come close . . .

Perhaps I have gone on too long with this, but if I don't get it down now I fear I never will, though I have become pretty damn good at it if you please. Still, K said more about Ananius than I can recall even after such a short passage of time, but I do remember he was certain the poet had had an unfriendly encounter with that old dog Diogenes during one of his trips to Corinth, which he could prove if he only had the time. It is all in here he said, handing me a package he had removed from his leather pouch, his work on Ananius' poems, at which his superiors had scoffed years ago, and which he was now placing in my hands. As I tried to make sense of this moment, holding the thick, heavy packet he had handed me, the waiter brought me the "Rechnung". Dumbstruck, I stared at it, my heart and mind racing with anxiety and possible responses to the situation. But K saved it. "Muß ich immer bezahlen?" he asked, and answered with a barely audible, "Ja."

As we left the Bahnhof, his conversation returned to the unfortunate Siegfried, saying perhaps his short heroic life was for the best. He was too soft, "ein μαλακός," he confided, the kind of young man who was moved to tears by the sight of some of his comrades walking along a street in Athens eating olives and spitting out the pits in the direction of a crowd of children, the quickest of whom picked up each stone and sucked it clean. It was immediately after Siegfried had told him about this during a brief leave home that K decided to bring about the change of scenery for him, to change the κίναιδος into a hoplite. Saved from having to respond to this sorry tale by our arrival at the taxi stand, I heard him suggest we now go our separate ways. As we shook hands, I thanked him as best I could and promised to write him from Cambridge. He told me solemnly that we were twofold comrades, bound to each other not only in "Kampfgemeinschaft," but also as two generations in the continuity of "Ananiusrezeption." As he climbed into his cab, he turned to me for a moment and quoted the famous proverbial phrase about the razor's edge from Nestor's urgent message to Diomedes about the fate of the Achaeans, to which I spontaneously called out the line in Chapman's stately fourteener: "Now on the eager razor's edge for life or death we stand." But the vehicle was already pulling away from the kerb, and as he leaned out the window he shook his upraised fist and shouted "Σύμμαχοι!"—so I seriously doubt he heard me.

I trust you'll agree that my immediate recording in these long letters of mine of K's unflagging and exhausting talk at me is preferable to any attempt to convey it through conversation later. This is more authentic and it will all be out of the way when we meet again. As the grey light of dawn begins to seep into melancholy Munich, I remain

Truly yours,

JB

#

[The letter that follows, from Sir Michael Sewtor-Lowden to Anastas Krebs, dated November 13, 1951, along with the other two items that precede it in these introductory comments, have been transcribed from their original typescript and manuscript versions by permission of the Sewtor-Lowden Estate. That this letter, collected with those from Jonathan Barker to Professor Sewtor-Lowden in the scholar's correspondence files for the post-war period, should be found among the papers of its sender rather than of its receiver deserves an explanation, even if the best that can be given is a hypothetical one. The letter and other items were placed in the file, presumably by Professor Sewtor-Lowden, in the following manner: the letter situated inside its neatly opened, stamped with British air mail postage envelope, addressed to Krebs' academic address with Sewtor-Lowden's on the back, with a November 14, 1951, Cambridge postmark; this envelope, in turn, situated inside a slightly larger envelope (also cut open along the top), addressed to "Herr Professor Doktor Sewtor-Lowden," at the same academic address as that on the back of the inside envelope, in black ink in large and somewhat wobbly letters, while the return address in the upper left-hand corner was printed painstakingly in small English letters in blue ink, "The Hotel Hestia, Kalavrita, Greece," bearing Greek stamps and a December 28, 1951, postmark from that town. Enclosed also in this larger envelope were two folded sheets of hotel stationery, with the heading "ΞΕΝΟΔΟΧΕΙΟ ΕΣΤΙΑ ΚΑΛΑΒΡΥΤΩΝ," each of which conveys a unique handwritten text. The first, and more complicated, of the two was written in black ink in the same unsteady hand as that on the front of the larger envelope addressed to Sewtor-Lowden, and reads:

—GELASSENHEIT ZWISCHEN—
Unwiderruflich, Freundin, bleibt mein Glück.
ΕΙΔΕΤΙΣΟΛΒΟΣΕΝΑΝΘΡΩΠΟΙΣΙΝΑΝΕΥΚΑΜΑΤΟΥ
ΟΥΦΑΙΝΕΤΑΕΚΔΕΤΕΛΕΥΤΑΣΕΙΝΙΝΗΤΟΙΣΑΜΕΡΟΝ
ΔΑΙΜΟΝΤΟΔΕΜΟΡΣΙΜΟΝΟΥΠΑΡΦΥΚΤΟΑΛΛΕΣΤΑΙΧΡΟΝΟΣ
ΟΥΤΟΣΟΚΑΙΤΙΝΑΕΛΠΤΙΑΒΑΛΩΝ
ΕΜΠΑΛΙΝΓΝΩΜΑΣΤΟΜΕΝΔΩΣΕΤΟΔΟΥΠΩ
Das Schicksal, das dich trifft, unwiderruflich.

.

Überzähliges Dasein/ entspringt mir im Herzen.
ΟΣΣΑΔΕΜΙΤΕΛΕΣΣΑΙΘΥΜΟΣΙΜΕΡΡΕΙΤΕΛΕΣΟΝ

The second sheet, carefully printed in blue ink in a hand similar to that which wrote the return address on the larger envelope, is a letter to Suitor-Lowden signed by Miss Katina Rigopoulos, which reads:

27.12.51

Sir Lowden:

Why did it you not say me you are in Hellas the 1927 with the Porfessor [sic] Krebs? Why? Telospandon, he is die here in Kalavrita, he try to go up the Chelmos, poor old man. I want to keep him here, but police say he have to go back to Germania. Before they take Krebs and his things, but I take these to mail them you.

> Because I know you read the Greek good—
> Βρέ γυναίκα τίνος είναι τά παιδιά;
> Βρέ γυναίκα τίνος είναι τά παιδιά;
> Τὸ να μου φῶνάζει yes
> Τ άλλο μου φῶνάζει ja
> Βρέ γυναίκα τίνος είναι τά παιδια;

> ΜΕ ΛΗΣΜΟΝΗΣΕ Ο ΧΑΡΟΣ—
> Κατίνα Ρηγόπουλου

To begin, it seems reasonable to suppose that Krebs received Sewtor-Lowden's letter in Germany and took it with him when he traveled to Greece some time between a few days after its delivery and his reported death on 13 December. He may have intended to respond to this letter at some point soon, since the letter and its envelope were kept, possibly for future reference, in the larger envelope, which must have been addressed in advance to Sewtor-Lowden for posting from Greece by Krebs after he had fulfilled the purpose of his journey and was prepared to reply. That this was his plan is plausible even if it is largely inferential; less so, but still speculative, is the explanation that his sudden death was the cause of his failure to respond, for his demise may not necessarily have been the only reason for his not answering Sewtor-Lowden, there being no guarantee against other personal motives that could have prevented a reply even if he had not expired. There can be no doubt, however, that it was Miss Katina Rigopoulos who, according to her own statement, took these materials away with her before Krebs' body and property were removed from the hotel room by the local police and submitted to the bureaucratic procedures required for their return to Germany. That this was possible may be traced to the fact that the proprietor of the hotel was a first cousin of Miss Katina's; it is also likely, if not completely verifiable, that she was contacted by Krebs after his arrival in Kalavryta and that the two of them shared friendly relations of some sort, as her brief letter to Sewtor-Lowden suggests. Though we will never know exactly what happened, we do know for sure that she held on to Sewtor-Lowden's letter to Krebs and the epigraphical sheet of stationery for about two weeks before posting them to England along with her letter to the Cambridge scholar by surface mail. Whatever the cause for the delay, the envelope, once mailed, would have taken at least a week, perhaps as long as ten to twelve days, to arrive at Sewtor-Lowden's address. As we know, he had taken a short trip to Paris in early January of 1952, yet there is a good chance he had already returned home when this piece of mail was finally delivered, there being no indication in his letter of 6 January 1952 from Paris to Jonathan Barker, back in Cambridge, that his housekeeper had forwarded it to him before that date, though there is no firm evidence that she had not. One would like to believe that when Sewtor-Lowden informed Barker of the death of Krebs he had no more information about that sad event than what Wilhelm Giesing had written him.

Equal credibility can be affixed to the conviction that it was the hand of Krebs that addressed the larger envelope to Sewtor-Lowden and composed the sheet of quotations by virtue of their mutual corroboration and circumstances. Translation and analysis of these texts, along with the Modern Greek parts of Miss Katina's letter, have been provided in the notes.

The egregious nature of Sewtor-Lowden's letter to Krebs notwithstanding, a certain case can be made for its pertinence to the reception of Ananios' poems if not to the poems themselves. Special thanks is due Mr. Keith Quimby, Esq., who heard Professor Sewtor-Lowden lecture at Cambridge during the very time in which this letter was written, for responding with sympathy to a request grounded in that argument.]

Professor Doktor Anastas Krebs
November 13, 1951
Department of Classical Studies
Ludwig-Maximilians Universität

My dear, good Krebs,
I write to apologize once again for having sent you Jack Barker without
warning and to thank you for receiving him and helping me make more
of a man and scholar of him. He needed exposure to a genuine "laudator
temporis acti" such as yourself, and so I took the chance of reconnecting
with you. He has returned to Cambridge, armed with your exhortations,
so to speak, and ready to transform the crucial places in his argument
according to your directions. Even as I write this he is busy-busy with
his revisions and the final typing of the dissertation, which he is typically
doing himself. He should complete the degree (I fervently pray you have
not prepared him to embarrass himself and me at the viva stage) before
the end of Michaelmas term. Yet another leaf is about to fall from this
aging branch.

From Jack's detailed epistolary accounts of your meetings, I can see you
are as volatile and voluble as ever. But, δαιμόνιε, you almost frightened
him out of his wits! And, to be perfectly honest with you, me as well,
for some of your antics exceeded what I had become accustomed to
in the old days. And it appears you kept certain things from me, such
as that bizarre Thucydides and Clausewitz thing Barker mentions.
Fortunately, nothing came of it, for it would have destroyed your well-
earned reputation. You did right, however, in giving him your researches
for an edition of Ananius, which is now in my hands, I'm sure you'll be
pleased to learn. I had no idea you were that interested in the poems of
A, about whom and which I possessed scant knowledge to begin with,
believing at that time that you enjoyed the playful role of being in love
with love in a dead language, which gave you ample opportunity for
your matchless recitations. I will not question your decision to allow this
work to lie fallow for so many years, for, as we all know, our careers can
play strange tricks on us. Whatever this work's fate in the past, I assure
you Atropos will not put her shears to it. A mathematical colleague
of mine here claimed Archimedes would outlive Aeschylus because

languages die while mathematical ideas do not. But we will show Mr. G. H. Hardy, whom our philosophical Mr. Wittgenstein took to task in the 30s, that there is still life in a "dead language" as long as the likes of us are around to give it breath. Suddenly, but not inexplicably, I recall the occasion in a village coffeehouse when you stunned and silenced that silly old priest who said Aeschylus had renounced his plays, by explaining to him that when Aeschylus ordered his epitaph he sought to preserve only the memory of what the man had done at Marathon because he was fully confident in the undying power of what the poet had accomplished in Athens. Do I descry a piece of the provenience of your warrior-poet-scholar business here? Be this *obiter dictum* as it may, Ananius, thanks to you—to all of us—will live a fuller life than ever before in our edition. (I have the perfect former student—not Jonathan Barker, by the way—to work for me on it). The desperate nature of your releasing Ananius into Barker's temporary care and reports of your poor health notwithstanding, I will insist on keeping you apprised of the work's progress and seek your opinion when necessary.

These memories of our past acquaintance have been very much in mind since last summer, when I was sent to Greece as the British board member and consultant to the Association of Martyred Towns. While most of my work kept me captive in bureaucratic Athens, I did spend the better part of two days in Kalavryta, which now joins Guernica, Coventry, Lidice and others in the Association (sorry to bring up the painful topic of the war, but, as you will see, it is unavoidable). In any case, being there reminded me of our meeting in Greece in '27 when each of us was on an "Arkadische Reise" (my first, your 2nd or 3rd?). You had already published your authoritative and daring work on the Corinthian battle of the stockade and I had just read it at the behest of my erstwhile and now late-lamented mentor, Arnold Gray (he died a few years ago never having finished his work on Euripides—let that be an example to us!), before departing for Hellas, when our paths crossed, providentially, I recall we both thought, as visitors at the Austrian dig at Lusi. Remember our first conversation? We had just approached the site from different directions and were both staring at those most pathetic, emaciated tragic-eyed cows by the crossroads, when you, having divined I was English, observed that these sad creatures might find their cure in a drink from the springs on the other side of the village. I still say it was unreasonable under the circumstances for you to expect me "to get" your allusion. But let me return to the more recent past. In Kalavryta, while I was interviewing individuals who had been there on December 13th of 1943, the day of the terrible massacre, an event for which, I know from Barker, you claim some expertise, I met a woman, the spinster daughter of a former mayor, named Miss Katina Rigopoulos, who told me an astonishing story. I was trying to collect information about some of the victims, something especially dramatic, and someone mentioned to me that Miss Katina had lost two nephews, the fraternal twin sons of a deceased sister she had adopted. Covered in the black weeds of Mediterranean mourning, this handsome, dark-eyed woman opened her heart to me (she was terrifically moved by my proficiency in modern Greek, which, as you know, I pursued despite my own professors' discouragement) and told me all about her older sister—Demetra— yes! but wait—and how a marriage had been arranged, rich dowry and all, to an ill-tempered man at least twenty years her senior in the market village of Mazeïka, which is also called, as you and I well know, Kato Klitoria, just outside of which lie the ruins of ancient Clitor, the supposed birthplace of our Ananius. Demetra, after six years of fruitless marriage and frequent public humiliations by her churlish husband, finally gave birth to a pair of fine blue-eyed boys in 1928. Now the first of the tragic parts of this tale that I must tell, just as painful for you I now realize as it was for me, is that Demetra died in childbirth, calling in vain upon her *Christouli mou*, his mother the Panaghia, and numerous saints throughout her difficult labor, only at the end to supplicate Artemis, who, as we know so well, would as soon do harm as merely turn a deaf ear to the cries of a woman in distressed childbirth who has fallen out of her favour. There was nothing the midwives and the doctor, who arrived too late anyway, could do, and her life's blood and vital spirits departed her body shortly after her bouncing baby boys did. They were baptized and named, at their father's insistence, after both of his grandfathers, Tassos and Vassilios. Too overcome at the time with their grief over the loss of their first daughter and older sister to argue against this demand, Miss Katina and her parents devoted themselves exclusively to the cause of convincing him to turn the children over to them. This he adamantly refused to do. Luckily, or so it seemed at the moment, a second cousin of his with whom he had quarreled furiously over the inheritance of a vineyard removed him from this world with one quick, well-aimed slash of the knife, and Katina and her parents came and took little "Tasso and Vasso" back to Kalavryta with them. The three of them raised the little boys with utter devotion, and when their grandparents died just before the war, their Aunt-Mother Katina became their sole guardian and parent. Now the second part of this tragic tale, as I know you have by now surmised, is that these two lads were gunned down with all of the other adult males of the town on that fateful day.

I am sure you by now believe you know the rest of this story, but you are wrong. Rather your knowledge is incomplete, for you do not know everything just I did not know everything, indeed, anything, until last summer, when an occasion of public service unexpectedly turned into the pursuit of a private interest. You must try to practice that most impossible of virtues for you, "patience" (do you remember telling me how your mother used to admonish you, "Die Geduld, mein Anastasie, Geduld!"), and hear me out. When Miss Katina began to tell me the sad tale of her sister, I, of course, immediately thought of that beautiful creature you and I met one day as we were walking from Mazeïka to the site of Clitor. She was like a goddess, lovely and lustrous, and the sight of her seemed to be meant specially for me, I thought—quite mistakenly it turned out, for Eros λυσιμέλις struck more than one man that day. Now I understand why you appeared to be so unaffected by her presence. Your dissembling was so good it even raised certain suspicions about you in my mind, and your sudden change in demeanour towards me barely registered when I revealed to you my liaison with her just before leaving for Athens and England—rather callously, I fear, with our phrase "making out like a Corinthian," which, you will remember, we agreed one riotous night best translated our favorite middle deponent. In fact, as I looked back later, trying to establish the cause for our drifting apart, I assumed it was related to politics and the war, and that you had allowed that to become personal. Hence my trepidation in sending Barker to you and my relief—but I get ahead of myself, of my ἀναγνώρῐσις. As I just wrote, I believed only I heard her siren song, and during those few days I kept secret watch for her and, encountering her the afternoon of the day before my return to Athens, obeyed her gaze by following her into the precincts of ancient Clitor to that ruined church with pieces of Doric column that you thought had succeeded to the site of the original temple of Demeter beside the Karnesi, with a freshly ploughed field on the far side bank of the river—hardly, I remember reassuring myself, what we would call here in England a "redundant" chapel. The presence of blankets and pillows, strewn with flower petals, on its floor suggested, for some reason unsurprisingly to me, that she had deliberately planned it all for our encounter. About which I will only say she made ferocious, unforgettable love to me like a woman possessed. The first time in my young life that a woman camped down on me and rode me like a pony. Now, if everything Miss Katina had told me provoked me to draw a certain picture, her firmly held opinion that the cause of Demetra's infertility lay not within her but her husband struck me with the force of a hair-raising thunderbolt. It suddenly seemed certain to me, given the timing and circumstances of my singular affair with Demetra, that I was the father of Tasso and Vasso! As I pondered this probable possibility and attempted to respond to my barely manageable feelings as one caught up in a set of tragic circumstances, I lost track of her narration for a moment, but hearing the words "Καθηγητής Γερμανός" I asked her to forgive me for being so overcome by her tale and to go back to her mention of the words "German Professor." This she did and what she said evoked a startling recognition in me. When it was apparent that Demetra was with child, giving her husband cause to inflate his chest, she confided to her sister that she was sure she had brought this about by seducing the German professor who was always hanging about the ruins of Clitor. Her sister had done this, Miss Katina assured me, out of necessity, to put an end to her husband's vicious and brutal fits of blaming their childlessness on her and her lineage, not because she was a loose or promiscuous woman. Convinced God would forgive her, Demetra expected to bear a beautiful boy to His glory despite her husband's lifeless seed, but her triumph, her double triumph, turned to vinegar and gall. Not because she died giving birth to them, for her sister claimed—and here her voice broke for the first time—she died, if not happily, knowing her younger sister would help them to a long life, but because these two handsome boys, whose extraordinary beauty would have brought the worst torment of self-doubt to their so-called father (had he lived to see them grow up), were so unfairly and irrevocably ripped away from this world. The German, begetter of her beloved boys, her αγόρια, had turned out to be the instrument of their obliteration. "Germani!" she cried, in a voice wrapped in profound and numbing hatred. At this point, it seemed to me Miss Katina began to say things of a nature confusing herself with her sister, but I had confused thoughts of my own to sort out.

"Eine Ironie des Schicksals" is it not? That we both should have good reason to believe these two boys were yours, or mine, or, better yet, ours together, each of us having scattered his biscuits, in your case Plätzchen, inside the tragic loins of the unforgettable Demetra within a matter of days or even hours? For that is how I conceive of this having happened, you and I going with her in a sequence only she could ever know for sure, though circumstances force me to concede the likelihood of your having got there first. As for her confessing to her sister about an assignation with just one lover, I believe that was clearly intended to protect her reputation, a necessity in her world even with one so close.

So it appears our only collaboration, thus far, has been at stud rather than in study, my dear Krebsie, though I cannot help believing that in addition to our availability our handsome looks and fine stock exercised some influence upon our selection. Yet it all came to naught. Sons we never knew nor knew we had . . . Still, I cannot but feel that all this deepens the fraternal bond forged at our first meeting years ago, a bond so worried and frayed by events beyond our control it amazes by its refusal to break. Yes, the gods' ways with us are truly mysterious and we cannot foresee our disasters, yet this bond will continue to hang, by a single strand, if it must.

It is out of this renewed sense of ἀδελφότης that I feel compelled to give you a better account of what happened at Kalavryta than the one you gave to Jack Barker, along with your work on Ananius, in the Bahnhof last month. (As you must have surmised by now, he wrote me wonderfully detailed descriptions of your meetings in Munich.) Please forgive me if I must now say that even the greatest of your scholarly achievements disclose a powerful desire to rewrite history, a proclivity of mind that may lead to dangerously errant conclusions when allowed to stray from the rigorous discipline of academic inquiry. Because I have only Jack's letters upon which to judge the extent and nature of your information about that terrible event, I feel obliged to tell you everything I have learned about it in my official capacity, not only as a necessary corrective but also because of its relation to the past we have shared, especially since that past has now been so dramatically transfigured.

My history lesson must begin, however, with a prologue in the form of a personal question. Didn't you have even the slightest inkling that having your delicate nephew transferred out of Athens to a part of Achaia overrun with partisans removed him from relative safety and placed him in considerable jeopardy? Regrets after the fact, which you seem to have experienced recently, cannot be counted. I suppose you were motivated generally by that idiosyncratic notion of yours about scholar-warriors, which is fine for the field of classics but certainly not the fields of war, just as I must suppose it was your incorrigibly romantic nature rather than calculations based on factual knowledge that led you to use your family connections to lift him out of a desk job in the capitol, the likes of which he would experience enough in his future university career, and to drop him into the wild beauty of the northern Peloponnese, to set his boots, as it were, into a land well-worn with the footsteps of the uncle he would one day succeed in academia. But your dreams, in effect, took him out of the bureaucratic operations of the Jew-hating Höherer SS-und-Polizeiführer of Greece, General Jürgen Stroop, and put him into the perilous anti-guerrilla operations of the 117 Jaeger Division led by the notorious Greek-hating General Karl Le Suire. To put it cuttingly as I can, my dear naïve friend, did it not occur to you that your Siegfried had a better chance of returning home if left to participate in the clerical phase of the execution of your Führer's Judenvernichtungsbefehl instead of being thrust into the carrying out of Le Suire's Vernichtungskrieg? Which, I ask you, would have been safer, to help administer the extermination of civilian Jews or to engage in war to the death with the Greek andartes? It is quite difficult for me to believe you were even vaguely aware of the risks inherent in your fatal interference. Indeed, and for obvious reasons, I trust you had but dim, if any, comprehension at all of the alternatives I have laid out here. But acts of hubris, as we all know, need not be well informed—because they never are—for us to suffer fully the terrible weight of their sequelae.

As for what happened in Kalavryta on December 13, 1943, and what precipitated it, I shall be brief and direct. (By the way, hardly any of this came from Miss Katina, for reasons you should well understand once you read it.) In a fight at Kerpini, several kilometres NW of Kalavryta, between German troops and Greek resistance forces belonging to ELAS, the Greeks captured and executed 78 soldiers of Le Suire's 117 Jaeger Division. According to the reprisal policy of Sühnemassnahmen, Le Suire ordered brutal attacks throughout the area and directed Kommandant Tenner to surround Kalavryta, where some of his men persistently rang the bells in every church until all of the town's inhabitants came out of their houses (the original clock on the rebuilt Metropolitan Church stands to this day at 2:34). After driving everyone into the schoolyard, the Germans separated the men and boys over 15 and herded them to a hill overlooking the town. Then, after setting the town on fire, they machine gunned the 1,436 males, whose last sight on this earth was of their homes and loved ones going up in flames. And indeed, the Germans locked up the women and children in the school and set it afire. They were spared, the eyewitness report goes, only because a German guard who said he was a father and could not bear the horror unlocked the door and was promptly shot for his trouble by a comrade. But the surviving women and children rushed to their escape, trampling one of their own, a poor old woman, to death in their stampede. It was left to these women, including Miss Katina, who said nothing to me about this most terrible part of her story, to bury and rebury their dead with their bare hands, attempting to thwart the packs of wild dogs who had picked up the scent of the blood and brains-soaked earth. What good the sacred springs for such madness? Your army then marched away from the massacre, their singing and yodeling an affront to what little light was left in the darkling sky, and on to Ayia Lavra the next day where they murdered whatever monks they found there and burned the monastery.

Such are the bare facts, Needless to say, most of your fanciful account to Jack hardly squares with them. Where on earth did you find the scraps of rumour upon which you based your reconstruction of the event? Chelmos stands in the opposite direction from Kerpini to Kalavryta, and your story about the commanding officer's younger brother sounds very much like an instance of thematic attraction. Because it was you who lost the relative in the skirmish, you were probably trying to justify your own thirst for vengeance with a personal explanation for the extreme brutality of this reprisal by secreting it in an imagined duplicate relationship. But I must forgive you, of course, for your failure to edit life itself as well as you have its written testaments, and I want you to know I deeply commiserate with you over the loss of your beloved nephew, who, had he lived, would be completing your Ananius work instead of me. The pain of that, in addition to your recognition—to what degree I cannot pretend to estimate—of your own complicity in the tragic chain of events that led to your state of bereavement must have been excruciating. Still, I cannot help but note, with some satisfaction, the small irony in the palliative effect and comfort my sending Jack Barker may have brought you, for yours is the greater loss, though now a profounder irony holds us together in its coils.

ὦ παιδοποιοὶ συμφοραὶ, πόνοι βροτῶν cries the mother Muse of Euripides' Rhesus!

Unlike good old Graysie and contrary to my own earlier view, I am now convinced these words belong to the great dramatist. Indeed even as the woes of childbearing have befallen Demetra, and Miss Katina as well, so too has this most fundamental grief of mankind touched us. We thought to live childless, never to bear sons to the grave, but . . .

I shan't go on, other than to assure you that neither the deaths of Siegfried and the twins nor your illness shall prevail. Gelassenheit. Your "Die Fragmente der Ananius" will see the light of day. Through all of this, have we not, in the final analysis, been terribly Greek?

M S-L

ENDNOTES

"God is also in the notes."
—Stavros Stavrides

Poems & Fragments (hereafter cited as *PF*)

1. See below, the first of the trio of "reconstituted poems" published by Sewtor-Lowden in the *Review of Classical Studies*. Cf. Pausanias, *Description of Greece* (*Periegesis Hellados*) 8.21.2, where the site of the alleged phenomenon of the singing spotted-fish is given as the Aroanios River. Since Jonathan Barker, in his letter of 26 October 1951 to Sewtor-Lowden, mentions that Krebs spoke to him about significant differences between Pausanias and Ananios, in which the poet proleptically corrects the travel writer's error, are we not obligated to infer that the text of this poem, if not those of the other two, presented by Sewtor-Lowden in *RCS* is based upon the transcription, interpretation, and reconstruction work of Krebs, the febrile quality of Barker's prose notwithstanding? We may also note that Theophanes appears to have been familiar with this poem in some form or version from his attribution of the phrase "the singing fish of Arcadia" to the demonic Ananias in their encounter described in our second selection from his *The Holy Book of Accounts*.

3. See below, the second of the "reconstituted poems" published in *RCS*. In the penultimate verse we find a reversal of the image of a traditional double herm, in which the superimposed heads are situated back to back and look outward; in the poem not only are the lovers face to face, but, as many *hermai* featured the god's genitals in addition to his head, it is possible the lovers embrace one another genital to genital as well, though this can only be inferred. Thus Hermes, guardian of travelers, joins Aphrodite and Eros as a patron of the lovers, directing their amorous journey to its final destination. I believe it incumbent upon me to observe that it was typical of Sewtor-Lowden's annotative text to become increasingly impertinent and wall-eyed as he moved from editing the poems for *RCS* to preparing the full edition by Grossmann. The following passage, which appears only in the notes to the book edition, exemplifies the manner in which he insinuates his learnedness through the casual introduction of the scarcely relevant: "The poet from Kleitor [i.e., Ananios] certainly knew, as we all do, the most famous story about herms, namely, that on the morning of June 7, 415 BC, Athenians found that the stone statues of Hermes all over the city had been defaced, their faces smashed and phalluses hacked or chipped off. Suspicions were aroused that this assault on the god of travelers was intended to achieve a political end by creating an omen against the fateful expedition about to set sail for Sicily. There were individuals who believed Alcibiades and his friends were responsible (Thucy. 6.28), but nothing much came of it. The perpetrators were probably just some drunken members of a *hetairia* determined on making mischief, but many Athenians feared darker motives, supposing Corinthian sabotage" (109).

4. Crow (Korone [Κορώνη]) was a common nickname for prostitutes. Nannion, a well-known whore who was nicknamed "the Proscenium" because she was so ugly after she stripped off her jewelry and clothes, actually named her daughter Crow, who was, in turn, nicknamed "Grandma" because she serviced three generations. See Athenaeus, *The Deipnosophists* (also popularly titled in English *Doctors at Dinner*) 13.583a,c and 587b. Perhaps this is one of the beginnings of the long road to Ovid's *Metamorphoses* 2.531–632 and Horace's *Odes* 4.13.

5. Despite the two specifics of topographical and mythological order, there is little we can do to make sense of this fragment. Not quite so its context. Kos, an ancient center of healing and site of a famous Asklepeion well before the birth of its most illustrious son, "the father of medicine," Hippocrates (c. 460–c. 370 BC), is one of the larger islands among the Dodecanese off the southwest coast of Asia Minor. It is unlikely, though not impossible, that Ananios ever visited Kos or included any kind of reference in this poem to Hippocrates, whose great renown developed long after his death. Phorkys, one of the earliest of sea gods, was said to have been the father, with his sister Keto, of the three Gorgons, Stheno, Euryale (see fragment 9 and note), and Medusa, and of the dragon who guarded the Apples of the Hesperides; he was also the father, *inter alios*, of the monster Skylla and of the nymph Thoosa, who bore Poseidon's son, the one-eyed giant Polyphemos, both of Homer's *Odyssey*. There is no known connection between Phorkys and Kos. Sewtor-Lowden's note on this fragment in his edition proposes "a possible thematic nexus" through the hero Herakles (though there is no trace of him in this sparse text), whose ship, when he was returning from Troy, Hera caused angry winds to blow to Kos (see *Iliad* 14.249ff. and 15.24ff.), where he fought with its inhabitants, who had mistaken him for a pirate. According to Sewtor-Lowden there is an account of Herakles killing Skylla after she devoured some of the cattle he was herding home that he had captured after he killed Geryon, but Phorkys magically revived her. That this act somehow affiliates Phorkys with the healing cults and traditions of Kos—or even begs a comparison with Melampous, about whom, "as we all know, Ananius wrote a poem"—ought not to be seriously entertained. Even though the documents containing the foundational work of Krebs on the poems of Ananios have somehow disappeared, there is almost as good a chance of our finding such lame speculations in them as there is of our filling in the gaps of this intriguing fragment.

7. Aphaia, a prehistoric goddess from the island of Aegina, like her Cretan counterpart, Britomartis, was dear to Artemis. Indeed, these two huntresses, "chaste and fair," share the same essential tale: King Minos fell madly in love with Britomartis, the gentle virgin from Gortyn, and pursued her for nine months until she threw her herself into the sea—in the Aeginetan version, he chases Aphaia all the way to Aegina, where she also throws herself off a cliff into the sea. By falling into the nets cast by fishermen, Britomartis is miraculously saved, given the surname Dictynna, "daughter of the net," and made a goddess by Artemis. According to Pausanias, 2.30.3, this virgin goddess is also worshipped by the Aeginetans under the surname Aphaia, who, they say, is the manifestation of Britomartis on their island. Aphaia was also associated with another virgin as well as with that virgin's parent, Athena and Zeus, both of whom were thought at various times to be the gods to whom the famous Temple of Aphaia on the east side of Aegina, or two earlier shrines on the same site, were dedicated. Considered the finest example of late Archaic temples in all of Greece, it was erected in the late 6th or early 5th century, earlier than the Parthenon, with which the Temple of Aphaia and the Temple of Poseidon at Cape Sounion constitute the points of a triangle used in an ancient communications system. Still, it wasn't until the 1901–03 Bavarian excavations conducted by Adolf Furtwängler that the temple's dedication to Aphaia was finally ascertained. In 1811, seventeen of its pedimental sculptures, figuring in Parian marble the combat between Greeks and Trojans, were found, or bought from the Turks, by the English and German architects C. R. Cockerell and Haller von Hallerstein of Nuremberg and then acquired in 1812 by Ludwig I

when he was still the Crown Prince of Bavaria, who sent them to Rome for restoration work by the Danish sculptor Thorvaldsen and then on to Munich, where they are exhibited as "The Aegina Marbles" in the Glyptothek. Like so much of the art and literature that has passed from antiquity into our hands, these sculptures are not without their own particular controversy. In their case, surprisingly not a highly publicized one of rightful ownership, like that surrounding the Elgin Marbles in London, but one that typifies the nature of inevitable disagreement among the principal agents of this passage and its all too customary disagreeable expression, as in Furtwängler's judgment of Thorvaldsen's restorations as "without much reverence for the pieces preserved" and being "the darkest hour in the Aegina figures' history." These were the sculptures, of course, that Anastas Krebs wanted Jonathan Barker to see when he visited him in Munich at Sir Michael Sewtor-Lowden's behest. The latter, master of the superfluous that he is, offers a long note in his Ananios edition on Britomart, Edmund Spenser's "self-fashioning" heroine of Book III of *The Faerie Queene*, of which no further account will be given here.

9. Euryale was one of the three Gorgons, daughters of the sea-gods Phorkys and Keto (see fragment 5 and note). Her sisters were Stheno and Medusa, and all three had the power to turn to stone anyone who looked upon them. Medusa, the only one of the three who was mortal, is the best known because it was she whom Perseus killed with the help of Athena, who held a polished shield above the Gorgon's head so that the hero could avoid her deadly gaze and gauge his decapitating blow by her reflection. This episode in the career of Perseus (see Theonaeus, item 7) was associated with Athena's traditional role as inventor of the flute, as in Pindar's twelfth Pythian Ode, in which we learn that Athena composed the first melodies for the flute in imitation of the dirge of the surviving Gorgons for their slaughtered sister, particularly "the echoing wail" of Euryale (20–21). Athena then made a gift of flute-playing to mortals, which may explain the reference to her at the beginning of this fragment, the last line of which looks to another chapter in the Greek story of flutes by its reference to Apollo and the satyr Marsyas (see Theonaeus, item 3). It will become soon apparent to anyone who reads through these surviving works by and about Ananios that he was habitually preoccupied, to put it mildly, with the subject of flutes and those who play them. Readers should note that the Greek wind instrument, the "aulos," commonly translated into English as "flute," was in fact a reed-blown pipe, usually played in pairs.

11. This intriguing little fragment starts us off with having to make a subtle choice between "deer season" and "deer cakes" in its first line on account of the truncated word ἐλάφηβολ- in the original. The difference between the two possible endings of –ion and –ia may be slight or virtually non-existent, yet one of them, completing the word *Elaphebolion*, would refer to the Athenian renaming of the month of *Artemision* (the last half of March and first half of April) in honor of Artemis during her deer shooting time, while the word *elaphebolia*, though it may well refer to the festival of Artemis during that same ninth month of the Attic calendar, could easily denote little cakes in the shape of deer that were offered during the festivities. Either way lends strong support to my reading of "Artemis" in the next line, based on the word-fragment –*is*. In his edition, Sewtor-Lowden prints the name "Britomartis," arguing that the mention of a "fisherman's net" later in the fragment justifies that reading through "a powerful associative image." Thus, what began with one kind of a choice ends with another, while we must still gaze mystified upon the beads of words strung through the silences that come between. Let us be thankful.

12. The last word in this fragment reads ἀν[.....]ον in the Myrsinus archive papyrus roll. Since this fragment belongs to one of the three "reconstituted poems" in *RCS*, see that section and note.

15. See Thucydides, *The Peloponnesian War* 4.133. This poem was one of several poems and fragments by our poet that were treated in a rather impromptu talk entitled "What Ananios Read And Who Might Have Read Him," given in English by the Norwegian classicist and film critic Ommond Gusevik of the University of Oslo at the State University of Illinois at Winnetka on 22 February 1969. Professor Gusevik declined the offer of Dr. Hugh Sydle to publish a reincarnation of his talk as a scholarly article in *The Review of Classical Studies*, which Sydle was editing at the time, presumably because of a sudden and baffling *ad hominem* attack delivered during the question and answer period, over which Sydle as host had presided. A member of the departments of Comparative Literature and Slavic Languages and Literatures at SUIW by the name of Dragan Markovich had risen to demand of Gusevik that he explain himself for what the questioner characterized as "your grossly casual and off-the-cuff accounting of author to author relations." Before Gusevik could respond, Markovich launched into a long-winded exposition of his own crudely conceived but boisterously articulated theory of proto-*intertextualité* in which one poet after another is said to have been "apsorpt" in an ineluctable succession of authorial assimilations. All this I have on the good authority of Dr. Diana DiSantis, who was a graduate assistant in the department of Classics at SUIW at the time. In a recent letter to me, Dr. DiSantis, who later succeeded Sydle as occupant of the Fylfot Chair of Classics, says that Professor Gusevik, trying to retain his composure and good nature, replied to this tirade by saying in his almost perfect (but for a slight Scandinavian lilt) Oxbridge English, "That was marvelous! You must write it all down one day." Shouting above the ripple of titters this response had elicited from the audience, Markovich exclaimed that whatever he wrote down would do greater honor to his subject than the shameful and outrageous things he, Gusevik, wrote about serious artists. During this phase of his extended denunciation, he held up a copy of the recently published English translation, which its author had done himself, of Professor Gusevik's provocative book *Singing in the Mist: Morose Lyricism in the Films of Ingmar Bergman*—the primary reason, incidentally, for the Scandinavian scholar's American visit, the original invitation having been proffered by the student speakers bureau to participate in a panel at SUIW's foreign film festival. At this moment, a young poet affiliated with the English Department named Marlon Olson, loudly demanded for all to hear, "SHUT UP, MARKEVICK!" As a result, Mr. Olson, with whom Diana DiSantis had been romantically involved, lost his adjunct status in the department of English at the end of that academic year, and Ms. DiSantis was tormented by an unspoken yet administratively palpable insinuation from Dr. Sydle that her teaching fellowship might very well fall victim to retrenchment. By the beginning of the new academic year, Mr. Olson had moved on from Winnetka to Brooklyn, New York, and publication of his first slender volume of verse entitled *To Die for Diana*; Ms. DiSantis had escaped the largely imaginary cleaver of financial exigency by agreeing to add grader duties for Sydle's Humanities Core lecture classes to her teaching load; Professor Markovich had been killed with his wife Marta, a painter and self-styled authority on film, who had tried without success for years to establish a fully funded academic program in film studies with herself as director at SUIW, in a tragic mountain road accident in a rental car with defective brakes during holiday in Yugoslavia; Professor Gusevik had returned to Oslo, where, realizing his career as a classicist had descended irrevocably into a moribund state, he abandoned academic life altogether to manage the family farm and write film criticism; Professor Sydle, who insisted it was "not within his purview (nor any other person's, for that matter) to censor, cut off, or otherwise control intellectual discussion," defended his silence during the Gusevik-Markovich contretemps and publicly allowed that the Norwegian declined the offer to publish a written version of his talk in *RCS* because he had already decided to jettison his "meagre career" in classics; and we, after having been drawn into this messy academic affair merely because of our healthy interest in an ancient Greek poet, will have to accept the silence that follows Gusevik's title with the same resignation and, if we are wise, equanimity that we accept the white spaces that besiege that poet's words.

16. The name Pyrrha in this fragment and in poem 15 might have been translated as "Red," just as Xantho in poem 17 could have been rendered as "Blondie," but for the desire to preserve the little dignity these poems afford their bearers. The most infamous Pyrrha, of course, has been gracefully demeaned into immortality by Horace in the fifth poem in the first book of his *Odes* (one wonders if the Roman poet was among those who read Ananios, according to Gusevik) and served up as an exercise in ventilation for misogynist translators, young and old. The word-play on "old me" in the translation reflects that in the original on *palaios* (πᾰλαιός), "old," and *ek palaiou* (ἐκ παλαιοῦ), "of old." If he were living today, Kosmas Logothetes might have included the translated version, though not the Greek of Ananios, as a perfect example of *homonymy* in his *Recipes for Rhetoric*. Would it be appropriate and fair to grit our teeth and employ a commonly made typing error to designate one who manages to steal a better effect out of his author's best effort a "translatro'?

17. See Theonaeus, *Games for Dinnertime*, items 3 and 7, for discussions of this poem. See also, note 9 above. The appropriation and psychological manipulation by Ananios in this poem of the Gorgons' devastating power to turn those who look upon them to stone—even when dead, in the case of Medusa—into a metaphorical representation of a love become petrified that recapitulates, with particularizing variations, its familiar source in myth may well astonish a reader who does not know better into rescheduling the dawn of romanticism. The reader who does know better will simply recognize the inchoate bloom of an anxious individualism.

18. Melampous, a healer from Pylos and the first mortal to become a prophet, had received the gift of prophecy when he was a young man from some snakes whose mother's body he had burned upon a pyre after he found her, a sacrificial victim, beside an oak tree. In gratitude for this act and for his caring for them, these serpents licked his ears as he slept, purifying them and enabling him to understand the language of birds and animals, which he used to foretell the future. We may note that a similar event provided one of the explanations of Kassandra's prophetic gift, the other, perhaps better known one, being Apollo's promise to grant her this power in return for her love. This line of Ananian verse refers to a specific episode in the Melampous story, a career rich in versions and variations in the writings of the poets, the Homeric scholiasts, and the early mythographers. During his effort to assist his brother Bias win the hand of Pero, the daughter of Neleus, by bringing as wedding gift the herds of Phylakos, Melampous, just as he had predicted, was caught and imprisoned for a year, and then set free. This occurred because while he was incarcerated he heard the worms in the beam overhead talking to each other about how long it would be before the beam, which they had been eating for some time, would collapse. Hearing one of the worms say the beam was ready to crumble, Melampous requested he be moved to another prison cell. Soon after, when the beam broke and fell, Phylakos recognized Melampous as a prophet and offered him the herd of cows on the condition that he cure his son Iphiklos of his impotence. This, Melampous accomplished and won the cattle as his reward, just as he had also predicted, turning them over to Neleus, who then gave his daughter in marriage to Bias. There can be little doubt that this is the fragment Barker says Krebs spoke to him about in his letter to Sewtor-Lowden of 16 October 1951. We can be less certain that fragments 34 and 37 (which see and notes) are concerned with Melampous, though there is room enough to stand up for the speculation that they may well be. Indeed, if they were, then the two of them, along with this verse, and the one quoted by the Anonymous Alexandrian (see item 8 and note), as well as the explicit reference to the legendary healer in the third stanza of the complete poem quoted by Theonaeus (see item 9 in *Games for Dinnertime* and note), the third such reference in all that remains of Ananios, suggest an uncommon interest in the figure. In fact, these three explicit uses of the name in such a small body of work (208 lines or partial lines and some 1,088 words) would argue, as I intend to later, in favor of the conclusion that fragments 34 and 37 dealt with Melampous in part, if not in their entirety.

19. For a description of the game the suitors in the *Odyssey* played, see Theonaeus, *Games for Dinnertime*, item 4. It is certainly worth our noting that the first view of the suitors Homer gives us (1.107) shows them involved in this recreation, which he calls *pessoi*, in which they symbolically play for another man's wife even as they eat and drink that absent man out of house and home. These days, the suitors probably would have had a board game designed for them called "Penopoly."

21. Made of pig's bloodstock no doubt.

22. Once again to indulge this specialized habit of mind that exuberantly wraps up its puns in parachronisms, we may imagine hearing a contemporary Ananios softly singing, "Olive Me, why don't we play Olive Me."

27. If we assume that this little fragment passed through the able hands of Anastas Krebs on its way to us—and there is no reason why we shouldn't—we may wonder if he was reminded of it when he read the message his nephew Siegfried Wenzel-Schott wrote to him on the back of a picture postcard from Athens, "Die schönste Zeit" (see Jonathan Barker's comments at the bottom of Sir Michael Sewtor-Lowden's letter to Krebs of 17 September 1951). We have been spilled into an enormous chamber wherein life continuously echoes art and art life, resounding through volumes of ironies bound in a plenitude of tongues. Some hear nothing. Others strive to link their strains to fulfilling termini in the cosmic din, transforming and modulating them thereby into a manner of music, or the illusion thereof.

28. Chrysosastros, according to this fragment and the passages quoted by Theonaeus (which see, item 2 and note) and by Kosmas Logothetes (which see, items 2 and 5 and notes), was a friend and fellow carouser of Ananios and possibly a poet as well. As this passage seems to affirm, Ananios' perception of Chrysosastros was at best ambivalent. The equation of the poet's expression of pity with his performance on a specific kind of flute for his companion's unfortunate accident outside a brothel introduces a topic that calls for to be continued attention.

29a,b. Sewtor-Lowden prints these two verses in his edition as if they came from the same poem. In his annotative commentary he speaks of a "thematic connection" and adduces a metrical analysis in which he scans each of them as "glyconic dactylized into the Sapphic fourteener" (x x – ˘ ˘ – ˘ ˘ – ˘ ˘ – ˘ –) in support of this editorial decision. Yet, he omits—we might generously construe to his credit—to state explicitly that he encountered these two lines as elements of a single fragmentary poem or even as written on the same fragment of papyrus, and for a very good reason, namely, that he most likely never did. Can there be any doubt that 29a is the line whose transcription by Krebs on a slip of paper figured in the accidental death of Sewtor-Lowden and which Sydle was asked to sight-read at the inquest, as narrated in the entry on Sewtor-Lowden in the *Index Nominum*? As the sole surviving piece of evidence of the lost work of Krebs on Ananios, this line comes back to haunt Sewtor-Lowden once again, this time for his overreaching zeal to unite these two verses into an exclusive whole of sorts. Assuming the sincerity of his conviction that the lines belonged to the same poem, we must point out that it seems to have escaped Professor Sewtor-Lowden's notice that two grammatically unrelated lines of verse in the same meter could just as easily have come from different poems, especially when one realizes that the theme that allegedly binds them pervades the writings of their maker. In the final analysis, whether they make a pair in a poem or not, all the other words germane to these verses that might have helped us resolve this issue lie, *in rerum natura*, submerged in the snowdrifts of time. In 29a, Ananios uses a form of the verb *Korinthiazomai* (Κορινθιάζομαι), which is defined in Liddell & Scott's *Lexicon* thus: "*practise fornication, because Corinth was famous for its courtesans.*" This must have been the "favourite middle deponent" that Sewtor-Lowden reminds Krebs of in his letter to him of 13 November 1951. It was during a "riotous night" back when they were both much younger and doing the classicist crawl around Greece (one wonders if Krebs recommended nursing their retsina or ouzo hangovers with the cabbage treatment used by Ananios and Chrysosastros [see Kosmas Logothetes, item 4]), that they agreed upon the best translation of this rare and colorful verb, "to make out like a Corinthian," a solution Hugh Sydle might have found helpful and I have been unable to resist. The word "Anchovy" in 29b is almost certainly the nickname of a prostitute or flute-girl, on which see item 3 in *Recipes for Rhetoric* by Kosmas Logothetes, who must have read the poem in which this line originally appeared. Since he was trawling the poetic waters of classical antiquity for specific examples of figures of speech, we should not make any inferences or draw conclusions about the textual homes of these two lines from the absence of any reference to 29a in his comments. Similarly, we must avoid being influenced, but with even firmer resolve, by the seriatim paraphrases of both of these verses in a sentence written by Theophanes in item 2 of *The Holy Book of Accounts*. Aside from the strong possibility—some might argue distinct probability—that he is referring to two different poems, stands the certainty that the "Mad Monk of the Morea" can hardly be summoned as a reliable witness in matters of textual adjudication.

30. In her day, Laïs was considered the most beautiful and desirable *hetaira* in all of Greece (see the poem by Plato in *The Greek Anthology*, VI.1). Some ancient sources say she was born in Sicily, but everyone affirms she spent almost all of her life, quite appropriately, in Corinth. Controversial, notorious, ever sought after, she was said to have had more lovers than any other woman. This epigram by Ananios, which confirms the story that she bestowed her favors on Diogenes the Cynic for no charge, is no doubt the poem Barker reports in his letter to Sewtor-Lowden of 26 October 1951 as being mentioned to him by Krebs. Greater credence redounds to the putative occurrence of this mordant encounter between philosopher and poet somewhere in Corinth from the reference by Theonaeus to Chamaemelon's account of Diogenes' biting reply in *Games for Dinnertime*, item 5 (which see and note).

31. *Schadenfreude* : Before the Germans, the Greeks, who always had one, as the saying goes, had a word for this questionable human emotion, *epichairekakia* (ἐπιχαιρεκᾰκία). Even the Romans lacked a word to denote it and had to resort to cumbersome phrases like *malevolentia laetans malo alieno*. Since it is the German word that exclusively supplies us with a verbal mean of acknowledging this sentiment, a state of lexical affairs lamented by Barker in his indignant letter of 26 January 1953 to Sewtor-Lowden, I do not hesitate to use it, one word for another, to translate the Greek of Ananios. There is a striking, if arguably inconsequential, parallel with a line near the end of W. H. Auden's darkly ruminative poem on the modern condition, "City Without Walls" (1967), in which an inner voice sharply interrupts the poem's speaker, "What fun and games you find it to play/ Jeremiah-cum-Juvenal:/ Shame on you for your *Schadenfreude*."

32. Perhaps this is the Ananian version of the expression to which the Anonymous Alexandrian refers in item 9.

33. It would certainly be natural, if not reasonably conclusive, to understand the referent of "old friend" as Chrysosastros.

34. This fragment will be discussed in the note to fragment 37 below.

36. This phrase could be the one the Anonymous Alexandrian has in mind in item 10, which see and note.

37. The text of fragment 34, which I reproduce below as printed in Sewtor-Lowden's edition, is the more informative of these two:

]θυγατ[...][......]α
]Πρ.....ς[
 ]σω[..........]ον[

In his commentary, in which he guarantees every letter read in "his" transcription, he proposes the restorations reflected in my translation (N.B., the letters at the ends of the first and third lines are omitted from the process). The crucial word, of course, is the restored name "Proitos," whose daughters Melampous saved from the curse of madness put upon them either by Hera for claiming they were more beautiful than she or for mocking her temple, as some say, or by Dionysos for refusing to accept his rites, as others say. In either case, the daughters of Proitos, Lysippe, Iphianassa, and Iphinoe, behaved as if they were—in some traditions they undergo metamorphoses and actually become—mad cows and run wild over Argos and Arcadia. Distraught, their father sent for the famous prophet and healer, and, after some bargaining, agreed to give a third of his kingdom to him and another third to his brother Bias if he would heal them. There are several versions of how and where Melampous brought about the cure, the major ones being the account in *The Library* by Apollodorus (2.2.2), in which Melampous enlists the help of the strongest young men in Argos to drive the raving heifers to Sicyon, where he purifies them and restores their wits, but only after

Iphinoe dies of exhaustion; and the narrative in Pausanias (8.18.7) in which Melampous leads the crazy cowgirls to Loussoi, where he heals them in the sanctuary of Artemis. In the end, Proitos yields the promised shares of his kingdom to Melampous and his brother Bias along with his two cured daughters in marriage, Iphianassa to Melampous and Lysippe to Bias, who benefits once again from his brother's generosity (see above, note on fragment 18), making it appropriate that we add the epithet *philadelphos* to the healer and prophet's name. Fragment 37, illustrating one of the papyrologist's cardinal rules that no scrap of papyrus is too small to ignore, may very well have belonged to the same text as fragment 34, for it not only strongly suggests the daughters' final transformation and recovery but also alludes to one of the elements involved in the cure, namely, the sacred springs near the temple of Artemis (see below, note on item 9 of *Games for Dinnertime*). Though the proposed complementary relationship between these two fragments may, and should, be open to skepticism, there can be little doubt that Sewtor-Lowden's alternative reading of "Proteus" in the second verse of 34 deserves none of our confidence. First and foremost, Proteus' one and only daughter, Eidothea, does not fit sensibly even into the most rudimentary and literal context presented by these fragments, and I cannot believe that the name of Proteus appears in the transcriptions and other groundwork done by Krebs, which I do firmly believe Sewtor-Lowden followed closely, though evidently not always closely enough. Krebs, we should recall, spoke to Barker effusively about the area between Loussoi and Kleitor as the venue of the healing of the daughters of Proitos by Melampous (see letter of 26 October 1951 to Sewtor-Lowden), a view obviously imprinted on his mind by the combined experiences of his travels and his work on Ananios. Sewtor-Lowden, who, we should also recall, thought of Krebs as a Proteus figure and referred to him as such in his letter to Barker of 11 October 1951, obviously could not keep Krebs out of mind as he worked through his work. Just as he failed, in his furtive way, to capture his protean predecessor and fully realize his secrets, we also fail to put so firm a hold upon this old poetry as to prevent it from escaping our will to possess it completely. We are none of us Menelaos, after all, nor have we been blessed in our educations with a goddess as instructor (see *Odyssey* 4.363ff.).

39. In the notes to his edition, Sewtor-Lowden identifies the source of these lines as a fragment of papyrus transcribed in a letter he allegedly received from Athens, signed by one "Paraskevas Kathenas," a Greek antiquarian collector and dealer, shortly after the publication of the three reconstituted poems of Ananios in RCS in January of 1953. He, Kathenas, had purchased through an "unlicensed Alexandrian connection" a small box of papyrus pieces and a few potsherds, among which he came upon a literary fragment attributed to Ananios inscribed with this couplet. In his letter, which was "composed partly in Modern Greek and partly in passable English," according to Sewtor-Lowden, Kathenas made a gift of the couplet's transcription in the interests of furthering the world's awareness of a neglected ancient Greek poet and invited him to make a fair offer for the papyrus in which it had been materially embodied for posterity. Sewtor-Lowden announces he "did not avail himself of this opportunity to become a party to such a shady enterprise" and, besides, he already had "the transcription of this elegant example of Ananios at his wittiest in hand." His asseveration of the couplet's provenance upon the authority of Kathenas—as if to say upon the authority of anybody— strikes me as utterly and outrageously, admittedly ingeniously, fabricated. It seems Sewtor-Lowden forgot that Jonathan Barker wrote to him the early morning of 26 October 1951 about how he had tried to decipher the singular fragment of papyrus among the working papers in the packet Krebs gave him, successfully making out the phrases that I have translated as "Hermes' lyre" and "with equal sweetness," which all but conclusively proves the papyrus with the couplet inscribed on it was definitely among the now unaccounted for missing materials Barker brought to England with him from Munich that fateful winter. Sewtor-Lowden's motive for permanently affixing this forgery of a tale about a letter from "Kathenas" onto the scholarly record when he had this papyrus fragment and its transcription by Krebs in hand all the time, must, in the final analysis, remain unfathomable. Still, I would submit as partial explanation of this unbecoming behavior the theory that Sewtor-Lowden, burdened with the knowledge that all of his labors on the Ananios edition were little more than an exercise in scholarly cannibalism, sought and found momentary release by feasting upon this concocted narrative in which he portrays himself enacting the role of the hero. Ironically, Sewtor-Lowden is guilty of an error of omission concerning this fragment as well, for nowhere in his edition does he mention or take into account

Kosmas Logothetes' *Recipes for Rhetoric*, which, in addition to providing otherwise undiscovered verses of Ananios, attests to the existence of this couplet (see item 4 and note).

40. That Ananios writes of Persephone's spending the summer months in the underworld with Hades should come as no surprise, for that was the earth's least productive season on account of the scorching heat of the Greek summer. This phrase, however, gives no indication of the duration of her sojourn below. Depending on which authority one reads, from the Homeric Hymns to the Second Vatican Mythographer and all who come between, Persephone spent a third of the year above and two-thirds below, or the reverse, or divided the year in half between the two worlds.

THE RECEPTION

Of the four early commentators only the first two, the Anonymous Alexandrian and Theonaeus, appear in the edition of Ananios published in 1960 by Sir Michael Sewtor-Lowden. Since the items following their names match up perfectly with the relevant passages in the commentaries of these authors, both of which have been published in *Papyrus grec recueillis en Philadelphie* [Darb-el-Gerza], edited by Traianos Giannakopoulos, volume 2, 1934, Papyri Societatis Archaeologicae Atheniensis, it would be fair to assume that the photocopies "of scholia and commentaries in Greek" that Jonathan Barker mentions in his letter of 26 October 1951 were of the pages pertaining to Ananios in this *editio princeps*. It would not be extravagant to infer from this that Sewtor-Lowden did not stray beyond the materials handed over to him by Barker for the preparation of his edition of Ananios. Indeed, we may find further support for such an inference in Sewtor-Lowden's demonstrable lack of scholarly pursuit of sources extrinsic to Krebs' packet. His oversight in particular of the publication of the complete original text with an introduction of Kosmas Logothetes' *Recipes for Rhetoric* by Joseph Gardane, "ΣΥΝΤΑΓΑΙ ΠΕΡΙ ΤΗΣ ΡΗΤΟΡΙΚΗΣ: Cooking with Gastronomically Poetic Devices in the Age of Justinian", in *Tracking and Teaching the Text, A Festschrift in Honor of Trajan Johnson*, ed. Gardane and Ellen Fremedon (Ann Arbor: Wolverine State University Press, 1956), pp.134–69. No circumstance grants excuse for this lapse, since the volume was available four years before the Grossmann edition of Ananios was published, and reviews of it began to appear in 1957, one of the earliest being a brief notice consisting of a listing of authors and titles after a laudatory introductory paragraph about the honored recipient by Hugh Sydle, then a newly tenured Associate Professor of Classics at the State University of Illinois at Winnetka, in the autumn 1957 issue of *The Review of Classical Studies*. (Is it not curious that Sydle, the fact that by that time he was no longer involved in Sewtor-Lowden's Ananios project notwithstanding, would have failed to pass on such useful information to his former mentor? More curious if he had and it was ignored?) It is essential for the record that I point out that Professor Trajan Johnson of the Wolverine State University's department of Classics and Papyrological Collections is one and the same as Traianos Giannakopoulos, the French trained Greek scholar and erstwhile editor of the extant works of the Alexandrian and Theonaeus, having legally changed his name after his marriage in Ann Arbor to the pharmaceutical heiress Madge Johnson shortly after his appointment at Wolverine. I delay identification of my source for the selections from Theophanes until the appropriate headnote below.

The Anonymous Alexandrian (see *Index Nominum*)

For the most part, these commentaries, which are more properly understood as *hypomnemata* rather than *scholia*, would seem to require little in the way of annotation since the quoted original texts (*lemmata*) that precede them provide specific literary connections or contexts. Still, we must be aware of the distinct possibility that these items tell us as much, if not more, about the Alexandrian's reading than they do about Ananios' writing, especially since we are once again left in the position of gazing upon phrases, lines, and short passages that have been isolated—I am tempted to say and do so, amputated—from their poetic bodies. Thus, in giving us one kind of context, the Alexandrian has deprived us of another, though the process of his reductions, unlike those of fortuitous time and blind book-worms, being deliberate and designed by an intellectual purpose results in parts that have been more wholesomely separated from their wholes. For these limbs we must be grateful.

4. The Homeric context of this reference to salt as a seasoning is the speech of Teiresias to Odysseus during his excursion to the underworld in which the seer's shade instructs him on what to do after he has slain the suitors, a passage in the epic that deeply impressed—we could say set off—Theophanes (see below, note to item 2 of *The Holy Book of Accounts*). In the note in his edition, Sewtor-Lowden, most likely following the work of Krebs, suggests that this line was part of *PF* 40, arguing the case on a metrical basis as well as on one of thematic affinity.

7. No line remotely like this is to be found among the jumble of extant verse by Hermesianax, who lived a century later than Ananios. Pity that the Alexandrian chose not to quote him along with Ananios, then again . . . Sewtor-Lowden comments, most likely second handedly, that "metrically speaking [a hideous locution] this line fits perfectly onto the end of the splendid Ananian passage Theonaeus quotes from Chamaemelon in *Games for Dinnertime*" (see item 1 and note).

8. Theoklymenos, the young soothsayer whom Telemakhos brought back to Ithaka with him from Pylos is "he who sprang from Melampous' line" (see *Odyssey* 15.225). A great-grandson of the first prophet (see above, item 18 and note in *PF*), Theoklymenos predicts the fate of the suitors in this, the third and final, prophecy he makes in the *Odyssey*. Our scholarly discretion demands an admission that we really know nothing more of the poem from which the Alexandrian quotes this verse than what he tells us, although that very restriction excites the hypothesis that it was once linked to item 19 in *PF*. We cannot, however, take seriously Sewtor-Lowden's supposition that the poem may have also dealt with Idmon the Argonaut, a grandson of Melampous and a seer, too, "who made the chilling prediction that his life was doomed by his choice to join the expedition in search of the Golden Fleece" (Apollonius, *Argonautica* 1.440–43). That would surely shift the focus of the poem away from what the Alexandrian identifies as the suitors—and to what purpose?

9. See above, *PF* item 32 and note.

10. Sappho uses the word *eumorphotera* (εὐμορφοτέρα) in 82a, pronouncing Mnasidika "more finely shaped" than Gyrinno, and then again in a highly lacunose fragment. We know the former, thanks to its being quoted by Hephaestion (130–169 AD) in his *Handbook on Meters*, and the latter, thanks to a papyrus discovery a thousand years later. Presumably, the Alexandrian had fuller and more direct access to Sappho's poems than we. His comment about the unique use of the word *orthotitthon*,

"erect of breast," by Ananios among the poets is confirmed by Liddell & Scott's citation of the word only in the *Anecdota* or *Secret History* of Procopius (early sixth century AD), in which the author, like the Lesbian and Kleitorian before him, makes an invidious comparison of his own, his being between the woman, Theodora, whom Justinian took for wife and the choice he could have made of any woman of the highest nobility and rank in the entire Roman Empire, "surpassingly beautiful" yet "still a maiden and, as the expression runs, erect of breast," (9.10.3).

Theonaeus (see *Index Nominum*)

1. If there is a single Ananian passage that inspires in me above all others a desperate wish for more, a desire that only waxes with the possible addition of the line the Alexandrian quotes in item 7, it is this one. Aside from the importunate hint that it was written in derogation of Artemis, which could have been a daring, even provocative, act, Theonaeus' wandering summary of Chamaemelon's comments confuses rather than clarifies matters, except for the valuable remark that tenders us the birth date of 399 BC for our poet. In its original sense, the word "holocaust" denotes a ritual burnt sacrifice, as the one to Artemis that Ananios describes here.

2. If Chrysosastros was in fact a poet, as attested here, it is so exclusively on the authority of the description of him as "fellow poet" just before the four-line passage Theonaeus quotes. Because Theonaeus is quite scrupulous about crediting Chamaemelon when he is in his debt for information about Ananios as well as for passages of his poetry, it is significant that he does not refer to Chamaemelon as his source in this item. Whether or not Chrysosastros is called a poet in some other part of the quoted poem, if, indeed, Theonaeus was familiar with more of the poem than the passage he quotes, is something, barring new discoveries, we shall never know. But see Sewtor-Lowden's note in his edition, in which he tries to make the case for this passage as an unfavorable comparison between Ananios and Chrysosastros as poets, concluding that "it is clear that for Ananius playing the flute stands for making poetry, and that he accuses his friend not only of imitating him but also of a deficiency in poetic gifts, being short-winded, so to speak" (144). Before we add this conjecture to the others we may have accumulated concerning our poet's apparent obsession with flutes, let us paraphrase

Sigmund Freud's trenchant remark about cigars and aver that sometimes a flute is just a flute.

3. The poem in question here, as well as in item 7 below, is number 17 in *PF*. The source of Theonaeus' allusion to Marsyas' cheekbands is the essay "On Restraining Anger" (*De cohibenda ira* 6) in the *Moralia* of Plutarch (d. 120 AD), though the famed biographer also wrote at length on Marsyas as an early flute virtuoso in his "Concerning Music" (*De musica*). Immediately following his description of the positive effect of wearing cheekbands, Plutarch observes that anger distorts the face and makes the voice even more ugly and unpleasant than playing the flute without the restraints of the leather bands, stirring never before stirred heart strings, which confirms with retrospective irony Ananios' portraiture of the nasty-turned little Xantho at the end of this poem. On Athena's invention of the flute, see above, *PF* item 9 and note. In another item in *Games for Dinnertime* 3.69, which has nothing explicitly to do with Ananios, Theonaeus provides us with some useful information about Iasios Lakon, namely, that he was the author of a work, now lost, entitled *Graphai* (ΓΡΑΦΑΙ) or *Writings* in English, I suppose, by having Kteson ask the Spartan physician about his meaning in a passage of that book. Kteson's question pertains to a statement he says the doctor made concerning the significance of Apollo's desire to embody the mastery of both the lyre and the flute. "Are we to understand them as female and male sexual organs, and thereby solve the puzzle of Apollo's victorious ruse over Marsyas?" To which Iasios Lakon, sharply replied, according to Theonaeus, "Cuntless wonder, look to your own impossible phallus!" That the customarily vigilant Krebs failed to see how germane this passage is to the item under discussion, not to mention the possible light it might shed upon number 39 in *PF*, as he perused a copy of *Papyrus grec recueillis en Philadelphie*, probably in a German library, may be astonishing yet must be true. Can we not be sure that had a copy of it been among the others in Krebs' packet, Sewtor-Lowden would have made much of it in his unmistakable way? Though we cannot know with certitude their sources for Theonaeus and Iasios Lakon, the stories that shape the discussions in this item are well known to us in many accounts, such as those by Apollodorus (1.4.2 and 3.10.2), the *Homeric Hymn to Hermes* (463–520), Ovid, *Fasti* (6.645–710), *Metamorphoses* (6.382–400), and Pausanias (1.24.1), to mention a few. The comment on the power of the flute to charm all those who hear it distinctly echoes Plato's *Symposium* (215c). If the Lakonian's idiosyncratic interpretations speak a special message to us, it may be that we should be on our guard against all those audacious discourses, beginning with those of some Greeks themselves, which would have us accept the Apollonian impulse stripped of all its dark passions and settled into a misleadingly easy so-called dichotomy with the Dionysian.

4. It would be pleasantly tempting to conceive of these two lines in combination with *PF* 19 and item 8 in the Anonymous Alexandrian as elements in the same poem on the subject of the suitors in the *Odyssey* if it weren't for the fact that no matter the pattern of their arrangement they would still constitute the kind of fragment that though it might be made to yield a certain kind of sense must yield to the ineradicable albescent state of its once and absent sense.

5. See above, *PF* 30 and note. Phryne of Thespiai, great rival of Laïs and lover of the famous sculptor Praxiteles, had the advantage over Laïs by having been the model for two, possibly three, works by Praxiteles: the renowned marble statue Aphrodite of Knidos, in a Roman copy of which in the Vatican Museum she lives on, albeit in a state of beauty several grades inferior to the original; the lost gilded statute of the *hetaira* herself on a lofty column of pentelic marble with the inscription "Phryne of Thespiai, daughter of Epicles" in Delphi; and a portrait in stone of her which once stood between the Praxitelian statues of Love and of Aphrodite in Thespiai. It is possible to assume the authenticity of Diogenes' riposte to Ananios' epigrammatic joke as reported by Chamaemelon and still not take its allegation literally, though trips to Delphi and Thespiai, as opposed to southwestern Asia Minor, for the purpose described by the philosopher would have been feasible, if off-handedly extravagant and whimsical. We can be certain, however, that the great Cynic's candor and self-inflicted humor about his habitual public masturbation was meant to insinuate grounds for comparison with what he considered the poetic ejaculations of Ananios. One can only regard Sewtor-Lowden's use of the occasion to re-tell what he calls "the appealing little story" of how Phryne, to whom Praxiteles had offered the gift of his most beautiful work without identifying it, tricked him into disclosing that it was his statue of Love, which she promptly chose (see Pausanias 1.20.1–2), as the kind of pedantic effusion the perpetration of which the scholar hazards regularly in the course of his lucubrations.

9. For a useful background for this item and poem, see Pausanias 8.17.6–21.3, despite the anachronism. As for Theonaeus' remark concerning Chamaemelon's ignorance of the "strange things" Linos and Epimenides said of the Styx, no writings of this sort by these legendary poets survive. The locales mentioned by Ananios in this poem lie within the area dominated by the Aroanios Mountains, the summit of which stands at a height of approximately 8,000 feet and is called Mount Chelmos by the modern Greeks. The spectacular falls of the Styx's source, the modern name of which is the Black Water or *Mavronero*, drops 600 feet down the sheer cliff face of Chelmos. Nonakris was a town no trace of which can be found today, though its ancient site was probably one of three neighboring villages in the vicinity. The ice-cold Phenean stream of melted snow, i.e., the Styx as it flows in the vicinity of the town of Pheneos, was thought to be deadly to humans and destructive to the material of all vessels except a horse's hoof, on which Theonaeus quotes Chamaemelon's note at the end of Ananios' poem and about which more below. Also very cold is the water of the spring Alyssos, so named for its quality of curing hydrophobia, in Kynaitha, present day Kalavryta, whose inhabitants Ananios succinctly describes in terms similar to those expressed at some length by Polybios (d. c. 120 BC) in his *Histories* 4.17–21. Born an Arcadian himself, in Megalopolis, he calls the Kynaithaians the most brutal, lawless, and savage people in all of Greece, primarily because they had abandoned the artistic and musical culture that was essential to their Arcadian heritage. The noble passion for liberty of the people of Kleitor was legendary (see, for example, Polybios 2.55), and the fame of their fountain's unusual powers widespread, especially as recounted by Ovid, "Whoever slakes his thirst at Kleitor's fountain, loses his taste for wine and, abstemious, enjoys only pure water" (*Metamorphoses* 15.322–3: *Clitorio quicunque sitim de fonte levarit,/Vina fugit gaudetque meris abstemius undis,*). Continuing, Ovid mentions its association with the healing gifts of Melampous, a parallel from which we might reasonably infer that the Roman poet could very well have read about this phenomenon in Ananios. Other writers making the same connection, however, place the spring in Loussoi, where Melampous cured the daughters of Proitos. Since the spring is actually located somewhere between Kleitor and Loussoi, which lies to the north in the direction of Kynaitha, Ananios either reflects the common view of its official locus in his time or understandably gives the edge to his hometown, a modicum of favoritism we can easily appreciate. Though the source of the river Ladon lies about three miles closer to the modern village of Lykouria than to the ancient town of the same name, the association of this deep underground spring with the vicinity of Lykouria was commonplace, as attested by Pausanias, who says its waters are the finest in Greece (19.20.1). The stories of Leukippos, who lost his life for loving the river god Ladon's daughter, the maiden Daphne, and Apollo, who gained the laurel instead of her love, are well known, especially the latter as celebrated by Ovid in hexameters in the first book of his *Metamorphoses* (452–567) and Bernini in marble. (By curious coincidence this translator's maternal progenitors, the Ananiadai, made their home the village of Dafni, named for that ancient girl-become-laurel tree.) The wines of the island of Chios were renowned throughout Greece. Sappho's claims for the two qualities of gold mentioned by Kimon in the poem to which he refers after hearing Theonaeus read Chamaemelon's note on the ability of the horse's hoof to withstand the corrosive power of the Stygian waters, are supported by the scholiast on Pindar's *Pythian* 4.230 and by Pausanias 8.18.5, respectively. Unfortunately, these two allusive traces to this particular poem by the splendid Lesbian are all that now remain of it, and Kteson's scoffing reply "that everyone knows that poem" must be revised for our time to mean, sadly, "that poem that nobody knows," though we can thank him for telling us one more thing about what the poem says, or, rather, does not say. It is likely that Kteson's laugh at Kimon's mention of Thetis' dipping the baby Achilles in the Styx expresses his disdain both for the late post-Homeric status of that legend as well as for one who would introduce it into what the contemptuous Kteson apparently regards as a serious literary conversation.

Those who have had occasion to consult the notes in Sewtor-Lowden's edition will recall that he mentions having walked about all of these places in 1927, "occasionally in the perambulating companionship of another classical scholar," and that the notes he made in his journal at that time have now proved most useful. Though he does not name this colleague in the field, it is likely that Anastas Krebs was that individual (see Sewtor-Lowden's letter of 13 November 1951 to Krebs). One of the notes he claims to have written then and reiterates in his edition pertains to an observation made by Pausanias, a copy of whose work he says he carried in his rucksack during his journey, in which the Greek writer perceives the irony in the rabies curing attribute of Kynaitha's spring turning out to be a counterbalancing good against the harmful effects of the Styx upon humans (8.19.3). But Pausanias, as is his wont throughout his work, writes straightforwardly here, remarking *without an iota of irony* upon a particular juxtaposition of springs with good and bad qualities in the topography of Arcadia, and definitely does not reflect a perspective similar to the negative view of Kynaitha and its inhabitants we find in Ananios' poem, as Sewtor-Lowden suggests. In another note, in which he fails to divine a real irony of a different and personal order, he dwells on the passage in *Pythian* 4 cited above in connection with the scholiast's reference to Sappho's statement about the indestructibility of gold, focusing on Pindar's phrase "the immortal bedding," i.e., the golden fleece, and extolling Jason as "a man of the hour sort of a hero, who knows how to seize what fate has placed at his disposal" (168). There can be as little doubt that the source of this reference was the packet from Krebs as there can be that its idiosyncratic application to the text of Ananios was not.

Kosmas Logothetes (See *Index Nominum*)
1. *Anadiplosis,* one of several rhetorical devices used in the construction of repetitions, entails the linking of two phrases or clauses by repeating the word at the end of the first one at the beginning of the one that follows. Pedanius Dioscorides (first century AD) was a Greek pharmacologist and physician to the Roman army whose book on herbals was the standard authority for centuries. The quoted passage comes from his *De materia medica* 5.1. Joseph Gardane, who edited the complete *Recipes for Rhetoric*, of which the passages pertaining to Ananios constitute a small fraction, points out that one of the key words Dioscorides uses, *kissosas* (κισσώσας), which Kosmas clearly takes to denote lustful feelings, can also refer to the special food cravings of pregnant women, which makes just as good sense in the herbalist's explanation of the virtues of the vine leaf's juice. I have translated it "women with unusual yearnings" to honor both possible interpretations of the word, though the poet's meaning that he fears the power of the leaf's juice to quiet his lover's passions

seems quite unambiguous. The source of Kosmas' paraphrase of Paul's highly influential contribution to western hermeneutics is Romans 15.4. The only record of a rhetor named Xydis of Corinth occurs here and in one other brief reference to him by Kosmas.

2. *Antonomasia* involves the substitution of an epithet or other descriptive phrase for a proper name. For more on the ubiquitous Chrysosastros, see the note above on *PF* 28 and the cross-references therein.

3. Kosmas may have read up on the nicknames of whores in the *Deipnosophistae* of Athenaeus 13.586–87, or in one of the authors mentioned there.

4. *Homoiosis* is the Greek term for simile. We are familiar with Rufinos through *The Greek Anthology*, in which a fair number of his amatory poems have been preserved. Of uncertain date, this poet is thought to have gathered a rather substantial collection of epigrams, including many of his own, which was eventually incorporated into the anthology known as *The Garland of Meleagros* (first century BC), the earliest collection of poems contained in the great compilation of over 4,000 poems by 320 writers arranged by numerous hands during the next several centuries and passed down to us as *The Greek Anthology*. The two lines by Ananios to which Kosmas refers, quoting only the first, are indisputably the same as *PF* 39, which see and note. While it is true that a poem by Rufinos similar to the one described by Kosmas appears in *The Greek Anthology* 5.36, it is difficult to imagine that Ananios wrote his couplet in order to insert it into the middle of Rufinos' poem, which reads as follows:

> Rhodope, Melite, and Rhodoclea contested
> which of them was best between the thighs,
> and asked me to referee; like divine beauty queens,
> they stood there naked, drenched with nectar.
> Between Rhodope's thighs shined the Cyclops' eye
> like a thick rosebush cleft by a western breeze.
> 　　　　　[two lines missing]
> Rhodoclea's was smooth as glass, a moistened front,
> like a temple statue that's just been sculpted.
> But wise to what Paris suffered for his decision,
> I declared a three-way tie, awarding the prize to all.

There are several good reasons why the Ananian couplet does not belong in the middle of this poem. That the first two arise from discrepancies of meter and dating would seem to obviate the need to adduce more, but let us proceed. The tone and imagery of the Ananios does not match convincingly with the Rufinos, and in fact the two lines read as if they were meant to stand alone as a discrete epigram. The subjective nature of these latter two arguments notwithstanding, the addition of the considerations that the name Melite was not uncommon and that Ananios was probably the earlier poet would seem to close the case. Gardane shows unusual ingenuity in his theory that "Kosmas was acting out a sexual/textual fantasy in which he enjoyed his power to thrust the copulative couplet by Ananios between the verfsified thighs of Rhodope and Rhodoclea, taking, rather than giving as Rufinos would, the prize of a rapturous 'threesome'."

5. *Zeugma* involves the use of a single verb with a compound subject or object. Ananios of Kleitor reflects the popular belief that cabbage was an effective remedy for hangover in all but the last of the quotations Kosmas makes in this item. Though we know this final passage is by the Ananios who was the sixth century BC iambographer, Kosmas obviously did not and was understandably seduced into thinking it was written by Ananios of Kleitor because of how easily the fragment can be taken as an address to Chrysostrastros, and its oath as a playful reference to their old standby cure for overindulgence, the cabbage. It is also possible that Kosmas' source was responsible for the confusion of the two poets, since Theophanes makes the same error at the beginning of the first item quoted here from his *Holy Book of Accounts*, which see below and note. To complicate matters more, the earlier Ananios, to whom only five small fragments are ascribed with certainty, was called "Ananias," as in the New Testament name, by the twelfth century Byzantine grammarian and poet John Tzetzes in his commentary on the *Alexandra* of Lycophron (285–247 BC).

Theophanes (See *Index Nominum*)
I wish to thank Professor Stavros Stavrides of Athena University, and formerly of the Phoenix University of Macedonia, for generously sharing some of the fruits with me of his remarkable discovery of the manuscript of *The Holy Book of Accounts* by Theophanes in the Vatican

Library. This major find occurred during the course of his researches into the history of the manuscripts that were removed from the castle known as the "Tremola," a keep situated on a rocky height near Kalavryta named after its first feudal lord Humbert de la Trémouille, by operatives of the houses of Othon de Tournay and Guillaume Villehardouin as the Frankish presence in Greece, which had begun after the fourth crusade in 1204, was coming to its end in the late thirteenth century. Professor Stavrides, of course, intends to write his own account of the fascinating and often thrilling experiences with which he met during the progress of his relentless (because it was perilous) pursuit of his prize, the *Codex Vaticanus Moreanus*. I, like so many others, anxiously await the publication of what will give the full story of this scholar's hunt of a lifetime, and thank my lucky stars that our mutual friend Professor Vassilis Vassilopoulos telephoned me from the Attica University of Ohio, where he had arranged an appointment for Stavrides as a visiting professor for a semester, to tell me he believed his former colleague from Greece had something in his hands that would be of enormous interest to me. When I arrived at the Attica campus, Professor Stavrides, who had been informed of my work on Ananios by Professor Vassilopoulos, generously gave me a fair copy he had made in his own hand of the two items from Theophanes printed here; at a later date, he kindly sent me a copy of the passage I reproduce at the end of the note to item 2 below as well as information to be used in the *Index Nominum*. As I have implied, the full story of how and what Professor Stavrides had to do in order to deliver Theophanes and other Greeks from the powerfully restricted zones of the Vatican Library will be his tale to tell in the introduction to his long awaited edition of this extraordinary codex.

1. Theophanes' first mention of Ananios may very well be to the poem from which Kosmas Logothetes quotes a line in item 2 of *Recipes for Rhetoric*, or a poem like it; the second mention, however, repeats the error Kosmas made in his item 5, attributing to Ananios of Kleitor words we know came from the first Ananios. The paraphrase by Theophanes resembles a passage from Ananios quoted by Athenaeus in *Deipnosophistae* 7.282, but that was probably not the monk's source, though we cannot be certain, as Athenaeus identifies his Ananios earlier in his work (3.78) as *iambopoios* (ἰαμβοποιός), "the iambic poet." Justinian's famous hymn on the mystery of the trinity may still be heard (or read) in the Greek

Orthodox liturgy of St. John Chrysostom, he of the golden mouth. Much of the wild and whirling diction that follows must have been based on John 21, especially since Theophanes quotes the apostle's notable phrase spoken by Jesus when he lost patience with Peter's questioning about his beloved disciple (vss. 22, 23) *ti pros se* (τί πρὸς σέ), *quid ad te* in the Vulgate, and while we're at it, "Wazzituhyoo?" in Brooklyn or South Philadelphia, while addressing a rock, *petros*, and a goat-headed sinner. The story of "the sardine hanging in a window" Theophanes draws and quarters from the Apocryphal Acts of Peter, the Vercelli Acts 3.13. The medieval name for the Peloponnese was the Morea because the mulberry tree, *moron* (μόρον), flourished there, hence Theophanes' reference to "the land of Pelops and the mulberry."

2. If one believes a sensible explanation for this bizarre narrative can be derived by examining its author's scriptural sources, one can begin by reading 1 Corinthians 16:19 and Acts 18:2, 11, 18; 1 Corinthians 6:9; Acts 9:10–19, 22:12–16; 1 Corinthians 10:21; and Revelations 3:7–13. That Theophanes was capable of conveying some details of his account with historical accuracy may be seen in his essentially correct observation that the Philadelphia in Asia Minor that was home to one of John's seven churches was later called "Little Athens." That city, the present day Alashehir in Turkey, did indeed undergo a period of pagan recidivism during the fifth century, which earned it that name for a time. Note the shift from the first to the third-person point of view beginning with the sentence "For Theophanes saw them there" and ending with the beginning of the sentence "After he had done this." Some may wish to judge this a symptom of a personality disorder, as if it were necessary to the proof that one existed. As for the Odysseus to Christ analogy at the end of this item, we would have to be satisfied with a simple reference to its rather common currency among early Christian and medieval writers, as in the *Gesta Romanorum*, 156, "De subversione Troiae," were it not for the good offices of Professor Stavrides, who has most generously provided me with the extraordinary passage which concludes *The Holy Book of Accounts* and in which Theophanes delivers an eschatological sermon on the mount:

> Do not marvel, brethren, that you hear me speak to you from the Aroanian heights whence the black waters of the Styx plummet to the lower regions of our earthly home, the black

waters the damned will ride at the great ending down to the earth's crust, piercing it to fall like so much rotten meat into their eternal infernal destination. Do not marvel, I say, that I have risen to this place where our heathen forebears believed their gods swore their blasphemous oaths, for my ascent has come about without my so much as climbing a single step, so great is the divine power that has uplifted me. From this vantage with my gifted vision, I can see the shape of the cross in a place full of the scent of pine and far from the salt sea here in the land of the mulberry where Odysseus planted his holy oar after he shivered the devil with it that asked him if it was a winnowing fan. For even as the oar signifies the incarnation and the cross our redemption, it will be as a winnowing fan as well to the devil and his suitors with which the hero will separate that chaff from the fruit he will cherish forever. For the coming of Odysseus typifies not the first but the second coming, the *Parousia*, of our Lord Savior as Judge in the company of avenging angels. Let those of you who have read the book of the life of Jesus Christ, the holy Eudokia's scared book, writ in Homeric by the Augusta who though born a pagan shames her who was born to the purple, let you understand and prepare to abandon your hopes for this life and look up at that fierce visage that bestows upon you your eternity. Be afraid, for you will pay dearly if you have got it wrong.

It appears from Theophanes' words that Mount Chelmos had not yet got its present name, and though he sticks to the name Styx and its pagan associations, his use of the descriptive phrase "the black waters" would seem to presage the falls and river's modern name. It is moot whether or not Theophanes possessed the strength and stamina to make the dangerous and strenuous climb up to the falls, and he wisely opts for an experience of hallucinatory levitation to get him, or to convince him he got, to the top. It hardly matters if we believe he actually stood there or just believed he did. His vision of what Odysseus did after he returned home to Ithaka and punished the suitors must have been based on that part of Teiresias' prophecy in the *Neukia* in which the seer's shade tells Odysseus to take up an oar after he has murdered the suitors and to go forth until he comes to a place where men know not of the sea or ships or the taste of salt. He will know he has arrived when another traveler will call the oar a winnowing fan, at which point Odysseus is to fix it into the earth and make sacrifice to Poseidon (*Odyssey* 11.118–30, repeated by Odysseus to Penelope in 23.266–77). Other than to guess Theophanes did not have a copy of Homer with him and that some years had probably lapsed since he last read him (but do we detect an echo of Ananios as the Alexandrian quotes him in item 4?), I would not venture to explain how this passage turned into the strange vision at the heart of Theophanes' sermon. That Odysseus wound up in the middle of the Peloponnese with his oar should come as no surprise, given the monk's propensity to reiterate the journeys of others in his own footsteps. Theophanes may also have been influenced, if vaguely, by the *Homerocentra* of the empress Eudokia (d. 460 AD), a version of the life of Christ told by means of a creative assemblage of Homeric verses, which was a highly regarded form of composition in her time. Eudokia, who was born a pagan in Athens and named Athenais before her conversion and marriage to the emperor Theodosius II in 421, was revered for her great learning and piety. No wonder she serves as foil in the monk's mind to his detestable Zoë, who as "Porphyrogenita" was treated to a royal Christian birth. Perhaps Theophanes was inspired in his own special way by Eudokia's radical linguistic and literary blending of Christian and pagan elements as he envisioned the Last Judgment and the end of time in Odyssean terms, in contrast to the prevalent tradition—outside of which Dante's novel treatment also stands—as reflected in the *Gesta Romanorum* in which the Ulysses figure plays the central role in an allegory of ongoing redemptive history. Theophanes may well have suffered from a "Pantocrator complex," as Professor Stavrides suggests with some humor, to put a name to that abnormally exaggerated sense of self that empowered him to deliver his weirdly meaningful final warning.

Sir Michael Sewtor-Lowden

From this point on, I have tried to keep the notes to a minimum, usually translating foreign words and phrases and identifying historical figures, when necessary, and providing sources of literary quotations, references, and allusions.

The Three Poems in *The Review of Classical Studies*

My first exception to the above stated policy arrives in the form of a necessary comment on Sewtor-Lowden's note on the first of these reconstructed poems. Other than the passing mention of Anastas Krebs in his brief introduction, Sewtor-Lowden's only reference to the German scholar in these *RCS* notes comes in a passage in which he recounts an anecdote he read in some notepaper on which Krebs had jotted down a few remarks about his interest in the poems and fragments of Ananios. Under the heading "Origo et fons," Krebs, in the words of Sewtor-Lowden, explained that he realized during his first trip to Arcadia he must find out more about the poet who seemed to anticipate Pausanias by writing about the singing fish in the Ladon and that it became a mission of great personal importance to him as he was then suddenly struck by the epiphanic recollection of a family story about his illustrious forebear, Johann Ludwig Krebs (1713–1780), the composer and organist and favorite student of Bach's, who had affectionately referred to him in the statement, "He is the only crayfish in my stream," punning on their respective last names in German, crayfish/Krebs and stream/Bach, in approbation of which some of his fellow students nicknamed him *der Bächlein*, "Little Stream." To this revelation of a purely human tributary to the wellspring of scholarly inspiration, Sewtor-Lowden casually adds that on "the sole occasion of a face to face meeting with Krebs" the latter, "with troubled demeanour," confided to him that Johann had been recognized as one of Bach's most trusted copyists and quite possibly had access to the master's musical estate. He had, thus, produced the primary sources for several important compositions, but problems of attribution and authenticity had also arisen, casting shadows of doubt across works appearing in the hands of both Bach and Krebs or with their ascription. Questions concerning the propriety, not to mention probity, of including such material in scholarly annotations give way to an entire set of new ones with the realization that none of this has been carried over to the note on this poem in the Grossmann edition. Sewtor-Lowden's allusion to Sappho 16 at the end of his note quoted in the text refers to a significant change in meaning to the restoration of the middle of the poem, the sense of which shifts from "Helen's judging Paris best who destroyed the majesty of Troy" to "Helen who left behind the best of husbands and crossed the sea to Troy" (see E. G. Turner, *Greek Papyri*,

69). As Turner parenthetically observes, "no scraps of papyrus are too small to disregard."

CORRESPONDENCES

For biographical information about Jonathan Barker, Wilhelm Giesing, Anastas Krebs, Sir Michael Sewtor-Lowden, and Hugh Sydle, see the *Index Nominum*.

Letter to Professor Joseph Fisher, 5 February 1952

Sewtor-Lowden's reference to "Graysie" is to the Cambridge don who was his mentor and then his colleague in Kythe College, Arnold Roundtree Gray (1869–1947). Gray's quoted remark is to A. E. Housman (1859–1936), the better known Cambridge classicist and poet in Trinity College of the same generation. For Armin Giesing, see the entries for Wilhelm Giesing and Anastas Krebs in the *Index Nominum*.

Letter to Sir Michael Sewtor-Lowden, 26 January 1953

In his mention of the absence of a word in English for *Schadenfreude*, Barker refers to Edmond Burke's 1757 work *Philosophical Inquiry into the Origin of Our Ideas of the Sublime and Beautiful*, part 1, sections 14–15. A suitable translation for *AEROLESCHIS* (ΑΕΡΟΛΕΣΧΙΣ) would be "Windbag!"

Letter to Jonathan Barker, 1 April 1952

The German poet Sewtor-Lowden quotes is Rainer Maria Rilke (1875–1926), "only Lament still learns," *The Sonnets to Orpheus, First Series* 8. Antigone's words are from Euripides' *The Phoenician Women*, 1855. As for the observation that Krebs favored the word *Gelassenheit*, one wonders if he extended its conventional meaning of "calmness" or "composure" to include the "serene renunciation" of the Rhineland Mystics and Meister Eckhardt, as Martin Heidegger did in his postwar ruminations in the closing chapters of *Was Heißt Denken?* (1954) and in the little book entitled *Gelassenheit* (1959), in which he redefines it as "releasement," a "letting-lie-before-us," a "letting the world world," "an openness to the mystery." Or what did Krebs, who strove to preserve fragments, think (or would have thought) of the appropriation of the sole word in Heraclitus'

Fragment 122, Ἀγχιβασίη, "going near," and its transformation into "moving-into-nearness" by a Heidegger striving for a new jumpstart from the philosophical energy of what he called the "The Great Greek Beginning"?

Letter to Hugh Sydle, 29 February 1952
IBC stands for the International Biographical Centre, JACT for Joint Association of Classical Teachers, two well-known institutions in Cambridge. Barker's Greek quotation is an epithet from the *Odyssey* 2.146: "far-seeing Zeus." Bassist Bob Haggart and drummer Ray Bauduc, both members of the Bob Crosby Orchestra and smaller jazz ensemble known as the "Bob Cats" not only composed "The Big Noise from Winnetka" but also performed its purest rendition as an instrumental duet (first recorded in Chicago, 14 October 1938) without backup music or the simple lyrics, the chanting of which by the band is included in some arrangements. It is impossible to tell which of its numerous recordings Barker heard that day or, indeed, how many different ones he may have heard later; that matters little, however, since they all feature Haggart's whistling and bass playing, accompanied by Bauduc's inventive drumming, which he sometimes does upon the G-string of Haggart's instrument. Barker's reference to the ox-hide wallet of Aeolus comes from the episode in the first fifty-five lines of the tenth book of the *Odyssey*, in which the hero's comrades furtively loose the wallet and release the winds it contained, undoing the beneficial effect of the gift the god of winds made to the homeward bound Ithacans.

Letter to Hugh Sydle, 30 January 1952
On the Temple of Aphaia, see note to *PF* 7 above.

Letter to Jonathan Barker, 6 January 1952
The title in English of this still untranslated study by Krebs would be "The Corinthian War: Towards a New View." I must confess I have not succeeded (nor made a heroic research effort) in locating copies of these Italian and Greek translations. Sewtor-Lowden's French colleague would have been Professor Marie-Pierre Folliet of the Sorbonne and, later in her distinguished career, the Collège de France. The patronizing gesture of providing the source of his quotation in brackets for his student would

appear to be in character. It would also appear to be in character for Krebs to expect those to whom he gave his card, as he did to Barker (see Barker's letter of 25 September 1951 to Sewtor-Lowden), either to know the rest of the sentence from Xenophon's *Cyropaedia* he quotes on its back or to be curious enough to look it up. In his note (to himself?) at the bottom of this letter, Barker has dutifully fulfilled the latter expectation. The clause printed on the back of Krebs' card, which Barker quotes near the end of his aforementioned letter to Sewtor-Lowden, would read in English thus: *for it is not just the duty of a leader to show his own valor*. The rest of X[enophon]'s sentence continuing, *but he must also take care that his followers be as valiant as possible*, then completes the admonition.

Letter to Jonathan Barker, 11 October 1951

Sewtor-Lowden describes Krebs to Barker by quoting Eidothea's words to Menelaus about her father, Proteus: "unerring old man of the sea" (*Odyssey* 4.384); the comparison, unfortunately, does not extend to the very next word at the beginning of the next line, "immortal," *athanatos* (ἀθάνατος), not even for the most learned of us, who may, nonetheless, seize the opportunity to compare what the writer of this letter says about how he first heard of Ananios with what he says about it in his letter of 13 November 1951 to Krebs. The phrase "broken-hipped lines" refers to the metrical term *ischiorrhogic* (ἰσχιορρωγικὸν), a meter ascribed to Ananios the Iambographer in which the *choliambus*, the "lame or limping iambic" famously used by Hipponax (also sixth century BC) for his invective and by the earlier Ananios as well, is altered by the addition of a third long at the beginning of the last iambic trimeter, thereby eliminating the limping effect of the substitution of a long for a short in the third position (short long *long*) of the choliambic; the ischiorrhogic, thus, employs four consecutive long syllables, an effect Jonathan Barker attempted to emulate qualitatively in the four consecutive stressed syllables at the end of the last line in one of his "Final Verses." That neither of the fragments by the earlier Ananios that are cited and misattributed to Ananios of Kleitor by Kosmas Logothetes (item 4) and Theophanes (item 1) exhibits broken-hipped metrics is noteworthy, even a bit ironic perhaps, but there can be no reason to assume those two commentators could have recognized, much less implemented, ischiorrhogics as a definitive or differentiating authorial feature. The poem by Johann Wolfgang von Goethe that

Sewtor-Lowden reports was recited for him by Krebs is "The Bride of Corinth," a composition from 1797 which indeed occupies a significant place in the rise to popularity of vampire poetry in particular and the Gothic romance in general. Its 196 lines, comprised of 28 seven line stanzas rhyming *ababccb*, narrate the tale of a young man from Athens who comes to Corinth to find the girl to whom he was betrothed by their parents when they were both children. The Corinthian family, however, has recently become Christian and the betrothed girl has died not long after their baptism, with a dark implication that the mother allowed the "bride's" illness to speed her way to heaven. Though he and his family are still pagan, the young man, who has arrived late, is welcomed by the mother and shown to a guest room provisioned with food and wine where he may spend the night in comfort. In the course of the fateful night, his beloved comes to him and, recognizing each other, they renew their love after she tells him her parents intend to match him with her sister. Plighting their troth, they exchange gifts, she offering him a golden chain and asking of him a ringlet of his hair. Despite her warning that she is a bride white as snow and cold as marble, he vows to take her home to Athens where the ancient gods are still worshiped, and he embraces her in his strong, passionate arms to warm her with his love. Suddenly interrupted and chided by her mother, the bride of Corinth announces her youthful lover must follow her in death and implores her mother to prepare a pyre upon which to burn their bodies so they may ascend with the flames and return to the old gods. Frankly anti-Christian in its point of view, the poem, according to Wilhelm Giesing, who devotes an entire chapter to it in his book *Goethe und die Antike*, explores the devastating cultural and psychological effects of the historically liminal situation in which its characters find themselves. Quoting the last three lines of the second stanza as his chapter's epigraph: *Keimt ein Glaube neu, / Wird oft Lieb und Treu / Wie ein böses Unkraut ausgerauft* ("The budding of a new creed often uproots Love and Truth like a loathsome weed."), Giesing begins his analysis by explaining that he first heard the poem himself at a transitional moment in his life as a young boy in his famous father's home in Heidelberg. One cannot help wondering if the source of that impressionable experience was not a recitation of "Die Braut von Korinth" by an excitable and intense young newcomer to the Giesing household. Likewise, it would not be farfetched, would it, to imagine two newfound classicist friends, tipsy with retsina, uniting academic Britannia and Germania in their jolly toasts and laughing at a joke one of them may have cracked about the *Jüngling von Athen* getting a big surprise when all he intended was to make out like a Corinthian?

Letter to Anastas Krebs, 17 September 1951
Sewtor-Lowden uses the German word for "charger," *Schlachtroß*, here to call Krebs what would be in English "an old war horse." *Urbanus et instructus* is Latin for "gentleman and a scholar," with the *semper*, "always," laid on by Sewtor-Lowden for good measure. The texts on the picture postcards Mrs. Barker had copied and sent me read, "The most beautiful time. Your nephew S." and "Alyssos": (printed in Greek) "It was fantastic!" See Theonaeus, item 9 and note.

JB's Final Verses
Dionisius Petavius (Denis Petau), 1583–1652, was a Jesuit theologian and teacher and the author of many books, including the two volume *Doctrina temporum* (1627), a revision of Scaliger's work on world chronology in which he originated and designated BC for keeping track of time before AD, but without the necessary and available zero between them, though the concept of zero had been transmitted to Europe during the Middle Ages by the Arabs, who, in turn, had acquired it from the Indians. Like all renovations to our intrinsically flawed program for temporal bookkeeping, the Petavian has made its own contribution to our problems with it, most recently the inflated and, mercifully, almost forgotten controversy over the inexact year of the new millennium. Naturally, like all people who lived before Christ, the Greeks knew nothing about the concept of BC, and even though their mathematics was severely limited by the absence of the concept of zero, the invention of which had an incalculable influence upon the history of civilization, their ability to enjoy life would seem to have been quite unimpressed by these deprivations. And one wonders what kind of sense the conviction that "Time is money" would have made to Ananios?

Letter to Mentor (Sir Michael Sewtor-Lowden), 25 September 1951
The AAC is the Academic Assistance Council at Cambridge University. BEA stands for British European Airways, a division, along with BOAC,

of the no longer extant parent company of the present day British Airways. For the inscription on Krebs' card, see above, the note on the Letter to Jonathan Barker, 6 January 1952.

Letter to Sewtor-Lowden, 4 October 1951
The reference by Krebs to Thucydides that Barker reports on the reliability of poets, rather the lack thereof, is most likely to *The Peloponnesian War* 1.21, where the historian makes an invidious comparison between his methods and those of the poets, who, he says, are in the habit of inflating the importance of their themes. The allusion that follows immediately to a "Walter" unknown to Barker is surely to the great poet of medieval Germany Walther von der Vogelweide (c.1170–1230). If Barker heard correctly, then Krebs was alluding to a famous poem of Walther's that begins, *Ich sach mit mînen ougen/ manne und wîbe tougen/ dâ ich gehôrte und gesach/ swaz iemen tet swaz iemen sprach* ("I saw with my own eyes the secrets of men and women, there I saw and heard what each one did, what each one saw.") While the rest of the poem can hardly be considered amatory in its subject—it is primarily concerned with the political order of Christendom—Walther may well be adducing his reputation for understanding human nature in support of his authority to speak on matters of worldly import. No doubt this poem made an early entrance into Krebs' storehouse of poetic memorizations. As for "Clausewitz," if and when Barker looked him up, he would have found he was Karl von Clausewitz (1780–1831), a Prussian general and writer on military strategy and tactics whose unfinished masterpiece *Vom Kriege* ("On War") has had an enormous influence on military and political theory— and of late (too late for Barker) upon corporate and business thinking as well as programs for personal improvement. Well-known for such ideas as the doctrine that every war should be fought as a total war, or as war being not merely an act of policy but a true way and means of implementing political activity, or as relying upon strategy rather than tactics to provide the foundation of every attempt to surprise, Clausewitz also wrote the sentence that caught the eye of Krebs, "If we go through the military history of modern Europe, we find no example of a Marathon" (Vol. 1, Bk.3, Chap. 8). The third unknown referent in this summary of Krebsian discourse, "the great poet's lines" we may readily recognize as Goethe's last three lines in the second stanza of his "Bride of Corinth," the very

lines Wilhelm Giesing used as an epigraph to one of his chapter titles in his book on Goethe and the ancients (see above, note to Letter to Jonathan Barker, 11 October 1951). Judging from what Krebs reportedly intimates here and states quite plainly through a literary reference in the following letter about his nephew Siegfried Wenzel-Schott, of whose death he also gave an account to Barker (see Letter to Sewtor-Lowden, 26 October 1951), Krebs believed Siegfried was homosexual. Thus, the sadly twisted meaning of his remark about the absence of a lion monument (and his wish for one?), when coupled with his description, recounted in Barker's last letter to his mentor from Munich, of the troop of German soldiers executed by the Greek resistance forces in the Kalavryta region as a "new Sacred Band," becomes quite clear. The lion monument to which he refers can be none other than the stone memorial overlooking the common grave of the Theban elite 300 man unit of hoplites comprised of paired lovers known as the *Hieoros Lochos* (ΗΙΕΡΟΣ ΛΟΧΟΣ), or Sacred Band, at the site of the battle of Chaironeia against Philip in 338 BC, only 46 of whom had survived the charge of the eighteen year old Alexander's cavalry. The victorious Macedonians were profoundly impressed with the valor and discipline of this force as attested by the disposition of their casualties in serried ranks, and allowed the special burial. They committed their own dead to a great mound, but burned the corpses of the Athenians and returned the ashes to the city whence Demosthenes, whose reckless provocation of Philip helped precipitate this momentous turning point in Greek history, had fled with others from the field of battle. Pausanias, who describes the site as the general grave of the Thebans and makes no mention of the Sacred Band, notes the absence of any inscription and conjectures that perhaps this silence was intended to address the discrepancy between the bad luck of these warriors and their courage, symbolized by the stone lion (9.40.5). Such restraint seems to have been completely lost by Krebs at this point in his life, having been quite subordinated to his inordinate desire to force a fit between the ancient and the modern. Unless he knew something that has escaped the historians, there is no way Siegfried and his fallen comrades could have qualified for the appellation he assigns them, much less a leonine memorial. Just as we may not avoid acknowledging that this deliberate absence of words remarked by Pausanias, along with all the words that have been erased from our texts by the aimless hands of father time and mother nature, gives us pause as well as cause to speculate, we also cannot avoid wondering what on earth a 1933 model of the SS (*Schutzstaffel*) dagger with the motto "My Honor is Loyalty" was doing on Krebs' desk in 1951. The truth about the how and why it got there and what it might signify will always elude us, just as the credibility of the stories of the murderous effects of the bitter verses of Archilochos upon Lycambes and his daughters and of Hipponax upon the sculptors Athenis and Bupalos partakes more of the chimerical than of the empirical, despite the attestations of poets like Horace (*Epodes* 6.11–14) and Ovid (*Ibis* 53–54, 521–24). Surely, we can see their victims swing forever in the nooses woven by their nasty iambic trimeters and lame iambics, i.e., the *scazon*, but can we know if there ever really was a gallows tree or crossbeam or window? It appears Krebs was attempting to slip a noose of his own around the neck of Wilhelm Giesing with this astonishing quotation, which Barker recorded imperfectly in his letter, from a passage near the end of the first book of Pope's *Dunciad* (289–90): by comparing him to Pope's grotesque hybrid, derived from a strange bird from Switzerland called a "Heidegger" (the reference to the philosophical man of parts and rector at Freiburg during the 1930s is immediately obvious) and an owl, traditionally associated with the cult of the goddess Athena. Thus Krebs taunted Giesing for having compromised his scholarly integrity.

Letter to Sewtor-Lowden, 18 October 1951

The volumes held as shields by the dancing-dueling office warriors are from the great German encyclopedia on classical studies, Pauly-Wissowa, *Realencyclopädie der classischen altertumswissenschaft*, which first started coming out in 1839, with the last of its 84 volumes appearing in 1978. Newer editions appeared in 1975, *Der Kleine Pauly*, 6 volumes, and in 2003, *Der Neue Pauly* in 16 volumes. Krebs, of course, would have had some volumes, if not an up to that date set in his office. The passage from *Faust* in question would be lines 4039–40: *Dort strömt die Menge zu dem Bösen:/ Da muß sich manches Rätsel lösen* ("Yonder the masses stream towards the Evil One: There many a riddle must be solved."). The brief quotation from *Hamlet*, is from the hero's speech to the Player, Act II, scene 2, 395. *Entartete Kunst* ("Degenerate Art") was the label the Nazi party used to identify art it considered decadent and against which it initiated a policy of brutal suppression, culminating in an exhibition under that title in Munich in 1937 in which 16,000 works were put on display with disrespectful carelessness and denounced in their inscriptions. I would guess with confidence that the influential relative was General Hans Krebs, first cousin to Anastas on his father's side. Ganymede and Ilus were brothers in the Trojan royal family, the former plucked up by Zeus disguised as an eagle and taken to Olympus to be cupbearer to the gods, while Ilus, ancestor of the house of Priam, became a wrestling champion and founder of Ilion, which eventually became Troy. My best guess for a source of Krebs' gestured oral quotation is Clausewitz, a stab in the dark, granted. Palmer D[avid] Slavowitz (1915–2001) was an unstoppable poet and novelist, all of whose publications have dropped into the pit of "POOPS," permanently out of print scribbling, a fate some of his translations of the classics may escape thanks to the alluring advantages of the public domain. Barker's recollection of Sewtor-Lowden's derisive remarks coincides roughly with the appearance of his savage review in the American journal *Review of Classical Studies* in 1951 of an anthology of ancient Greek drama, the editorial oversight of which Slavowitz somehow persuaded the distinguished press of Quaker State University to entrust to him.

Letter to Sewtor-Lowden, 26 October 1951
See above, the note on *PF 39* for more about Barker's attempt to decipher this fragment of papyrus in Krebs' packet. The quotation on Wilhelm Giesing's office door is from Goethe's *Faust*, Part One 3363 and is spoken by Faust: "Let what must happen, happen right away!" In order to hear Ludwig Wittgenstein (1889–1951) perform Schubert's 'The Trout' and other songs to the piano accompaniment of his friend David Pinsent, Krebs would have had to have visited Cambridge around 1912, at which time he would have been twenty-nine rather than in "his early 20s," assuming Barker heard or remembered his words correctly. Since he mentions it specifically, one may wonder if the nascent philosopher's whistling of the beginning of *Die Forelle* brought to his German auditor's mind the song's incipit, *In einem Bächlein helle* ("In a little stream so clear"), thus awakening in him a remembrance of his musical ancestor as well as of home. Goethe's *Triumvirn*, as he refers to them in the last line of his *Römische Elegien* 5, were the three Roman love poets Catullus,

Tibullus, and Propertius. This poem, one of group of poems also known as Goethe's *Erotica Romana*, was written during his famous "Italienische Reise", a sojourn of twenty months beginning in September of 1786 in which the thirty-seven year old poet underwent a powerful rebirth. It vividly depicts the poet's profound experience of an achieved unity in him of the worlds of life and art, past and present, through the single word *Amor* and its palindrome *Roma*. Since Krebs is indubitably thinking about *Romische Elegien* 5 at the moment he drums his fingers on the table, this action might well be (if I may) a sub-self-conscious gesture articulated out of sympathy with his retention of this poem in his memory, particularly the last few lines, in which Goethe explains that he often composes poetry while in his beloved's embrace, counting out his hexameters by tapping them on her back with his fingers as she sleeps: *Oftmals hab ich auch schon in ihren Armen gedichtet / Und des Hexameters Maß leise mit fingernder Hand / Ihr auf den Rücken gezählt.* In the midst of this outpouring of emotional reminiscences, let us not lose sight of the significance of its underlying context, an event, evidently of amorous import, which occurred during Krebs' 1927 journey to Arcadia when he was forty-four years of age. With the references to Goethe's fifth *Roman Elegy* and the partial quotations that Barker was able to retrieve from the ordeal in the Bahnhof from Rilke's *Duino Elegies* 9. 16–17, "Once, just once [to have been on *earth just once*]—the 'something or other' being *scheint nicht widerrufbar*—that seems irrevocable," and the plaintive cry of Goethe's Corinthian bride to her hardened mother, "Mother! Mother!" [she speaks in a hollow voice, / "So do you begrudge me] this beautiful night!" (155–56), serving as the bookends between which Krebs rambles through his memories of what he has seen and read about Kleitor's surroundings (see also Pausanias 8.21.2,4), we may find it difficult not to infer that the German scholar responded to the intellectual and intersexual effect upon him of these imagined literary correspondences by recording this memory as a crucial self-defining moment in his life's text. A case of *ars vitam edidit*, not unlike the ending of Sappho' s fragment 58, in which the Lesbian poet seems to proclaim the affirming power of love upon her life through the figure of the sun's light. Juxtaposed with Goethe's shimmering with meaning night, Sappho's solar bright symbolism illustrates once again the poetical antipodes of classicism and romanticism. Continuing with the references in this Krebsian travelogue and informal history, see Pausanias 8.19.1 on the Kynaithaians statue of Zeus at Olympia, 8.21.3 on the bronze statues of the Dioskouroi (Kastor and Polydeukes, the twin sons fathered upon Leda by Zeus in one version, or by Zeus and Tyndareus in another) just outside of Kleitor, and Polybios 4.18 for the Aetolian attack on Kynaitha. Thucydides reports the execution of the men of Melos at the end of his extraordinary interlude known as "The Melian Dialogue" in *The Peloponnesian War* 5.84–116. Krebs' allusion to Clausewitz must be to *Vom Kriege* 3.4, where the philopolemicist explains that a mountainous environment is highly conducive to the expression of "national spirit" through *Volkskrieg*, "the people's war," i.e., guerrilla warfare. The Austrian excavations at Loussoi took place in 1901; for Melampous and the daughters of Proitos, see above, the notes on *PF* 18 and 37. Krebs' reference to the medicine man's black feet is based on the eponymous meaning of his name, as explained in the tale of his mother having put him in the shade after he was born but inadvertently leaving his feet in the sun. The reference to Pindar is probably to a "skolion" (an after-dinner drinking song) composed in conjunction with, though after, *Olympian* 13, in which Pindar celebrates Xenophon of Corinth's twin victories in the "stadion," a short footrace of about 200 yards, and the "pentathlon" on the same day in 464 BC. In the last passage of the fragmented skolion *For Xenophon of Corinth*, Pindar records the victor's making good on his promise to Aphrodite, made before the competition, to donate a hundred young prostitutes to her temple in Corinth in exchange for her ensuring his success in the games: "brought into Aphrodite's sacred grove a herd of a hundred girls to graze, in gladness that his prayers have been answered" (17–20). According to the earlier passages of the work, the very same one hundred young women participated in the celebration of their gifting to love's goddess. While all this may seem remarkable, vows to make significant contributions to divine patrons in return for athletic success in the games was fairly common and not so very different, when all is said and done, from diverse subsequent religious practices. But is it not truly remarkable that Krebs could quote from "The Scholars," William Butler Yeats's acerbic poem of 1917, and aspire, despite his bald head, to walk the way of the poet rather than that of the editor, his intransigent temperament turning the Yeats poem to its own purpose? To which it seems he believed he had enlisted young Barker as the hoplite in place of Siegfried, the *kinaidos* (homosexual), as his departing exhortation to him was *Symmachoi* ("allies"), just after reciting the famous "razor's edge" passage, *epi ksirou histatai akmes* (ἐπὶ ξυροῦ ἵσταται ἀκμῆς), from the *Iliad* 10.173–74.

Prefatory Note to the Letter to Anastas Krebs, 13 November 1951
The handwritten heading "Gelassenheit Zwischen," as if announcing the Scylla and Charybdis like straits of delusions of happiness and fate through which its writer must navigate successfully to arrive at a state of peace of mind, reproduces first a passage from Pindar's twelfth *Pythian Ode,* 28–32, printed without spacing or punctuation but with line breaks in partial emulation of the *scriptio continua* in which papyrus texts were written, said passage being bracketed between two, originally consecutive but separated here, lines from Goethe's play *Die Natürliche Tochter* ("The Natural Daughter"), which was first staged in Weimar on April 2, 1803. These two lines are the last spoken at the end of the second act (1145–46), with Eugenia, the Duke's illegitimate daughter, overconfidently maintaining to her Governess her belief in her own good luck, "Irrevocable, my friend, remains my good fortune," to which the Governess, who knows more than her charge about the perilous situation of the girl, replies in an aside: "The fate that strikes you down, irrevocable." Critics have described this moment in the drama as one in which hubris turns into tragedy, and identify its rhetorical order as chiasmus, a term that didn't see the light of day until the late nineteenth century; an ancient rhetor would have simply called it an example of *epanalepsis.* Either way, Krebs spread these lines apart, like a Sheela-na-Gig her vulva, to fit the Pindaric passage between them: "If there is such a thing as human happiness, it does not happen without hard work; a god can bring it about this same day—what is fated cannot be escaped––but that time will come which, striking a man by surprise, will, beyond expectations, give one thing but hold back another." There is a notable difference between this new, highly universalized context for the passage and its original one in Pindar's paean to the victory in flute playing by Midas of Acragas in 490 BC, where these last four verses of the brief ode may well apply, as an ancient scholiast asserts, to Midas' winning the prize by playing through an accident in which his mouthpiece broke during the competition. This is the same ode in which a few lines before this, Pindar alludes to Athena's invention of the flute (see above, note

on *PF* 9). The second pair of German and Greek quotations come from Rilke's *Duino Elegies* 9.79–80: "Superfluity of being springs up in my heart" and Sappho 1.26–27: "all that my heart longs to fulfill, fulfill," this time with no line break. A curious resonance emanates from the next few words with which Sappho brings this prayer to Aphrodite, the only complete poem of hers to survive, to a close with a final exhortation, "be my ally," *symmachos esso* (σύμμαχος ἔσσο). The word "telospandon," which Miss Katina Rigopoulos interjects in her letter to Sewtor-Lowden, means "well, finally" or "anyway" in Greek, no doubt used by her because she did not know its English equivalent and with confidence that its reader would understand it. The little song she offers him was a popular bit of humor, albeit with a point, after World War II, transcribed and translated thus: *Vre gynaika tinos einai ta paideia?* (repeated as the second and fifth lines) *To'na mou fonazei* yes / *T'allo mou fonazei* ja. "Won't you tell me lady / Who's the father of your baby / Won't you tell me lady / Who's the father of your baby / The one cries "yes" / The other cries "ja" / Won't you tell me lady / Who's your baby's pa?" The wistful phrase Miss Katina uses above her signature, *Me lismonise o charos*, "Death has forgotten about me," was emended, I have been informed by relatives in the locale, nine years later.

The Letter

The source of the complimentary expression, *laudator temporis acti*, an appellation for praisers of the past, is Horace's *Ars Poetica*, 173. But matters are not so simple when Sewtor-Lowden addresses Krebs as *daimonie*, for the word, in its several forms and related parts of speech, can mean various things and just how we are to take it depends upon its context. While the word in Homer, where it is used in the vocative (as it is here) only, can denote a positive "noble sir" or a reproachful "wretch," or, as we shall see, "strange man" or "woman," in later Greek it can be used with irony, as in "my good sir" or "my fine fellow," or for the "genius" of Socrates in the *Apology* 40a and other Platonic dialogues, or for an "evil spirit" or "demon" in the *New Testament*, not to overlook the common meanings of "deity," "god," or a human being possessed by one. All of these definitions, and more, were reviewed by Sewtor-Lowden in his provocative and controversial early article, "When Penelope Knows It's Odysseus: Recognition Within the Divine Triangle," published in

1929 in *Zeitschrift für klasssiche Philologie*, a journal published in Munich, on whose editorial board Anastas Krebs was serving at that time. To allow those who may wish to follow for themselves the author's scrupulously argued thesis that Penelope recognized Odysseus well before any of the junctures in the narrative that received opinion has her doing so, we will consider only the place late in the article in which Sewtor-Lowden, intent upon making the decisively summary point that a benevolent daimonic power pervades and directs the couple's awareness of each other throughout the homecoming scenes of the *Odyssey*, pounces upon the two speeches in the twenty-third book in which husband and wife address each other sharply by the word *daimonie* within a span of nine lines (23.166 and 174). Their mutual name calling in this scene, which is unique for its soon to pass angry scolding tone, has been most frequently rendered by English translators, as Sewtor-Lowden disapprovingly points out and I can unofficially confirm, as "Strange woman" and "Strange man," or some similar wording. His objection is not so much to the specific translation choice as to the inability of our language to register the range of meanings offered by the Greek, whereby we can simultaneously understand why Odysseus and Penelope call each other "strange," what they may mean by it, and also grasp the poet's deeper signification of each of them having been possessed or come under the influence of a god, in this case that of the goddess Athena. It is she who in her interaction with each of them creates the state of "divine triangulation through which their relationship is informed with the supernatural as far as humanly possible and rises to a condition above all others of its kind" (138). It must be admitted that this essay represents some of Sewtor-Lowden's most original and arresting scholarly criticism and seems to anticipate what were to become rather standard approaches in a few decades; most remarkable, however, is the resonant quality of some of his observations about translation issues to the positions on that subject articulated by Walter Benjamin in what would one day become a revered essay, "The Task of the Translator" (*Die Aufgabe des Übersetzers*), first published in 1923. At a crucial point in which Benjamin dwells on the question of the need to come to terms with "the foreignness of languages" when thinking about translation, he writes, "The original cannot enter there in its entirety, but what does appear in this region is that element in a translation which goes beyond transmittal of subject matter. This nucleus is best defined as that element in the translation which does not lend itself to a further translation." Thus, when Sewtor-Lowden addresses Krebs as δαιμόνιε in his letter, he may well be offering, consciously or subconsciously, a name of protean, untranslatable proportions to suit the memory of a man who occupies—we cannot deny—a place of admiration and ambivalent sentiments in his mind. We know much less about his relationship with his "mathematical colleague," Godfrey Harold Hardy (1877–1947), to whose *A Mathematician's Apology* he refers here. One of the leading mathematicians of his generation, Hardy was educated at Cambridge and taught there most of his professional career. Though Hardy was a friend of many years, Wittgenstein attacked him, among others, for what he considered his deleterious influence on students of contemporary mathematics. In his lectures during the academic year of 1932–33, he read passages aloud to his class from Hardy's *A Course in Pure Mathematics*, then the standard textbook, as he vented his fury against some of its basic assumptions. It is believed Aeschylus composed his own epitaph, in which he omits mention of his literary achievements and refers only to his having fought at Marathon. The exact nature of "the allusion" that Krebs made and Sewtor-Lowden did not "get" at their fortuitous first encounter we can only guess at. Perhaps it was simply to the springs sacred to Artemis situated between Kleitor and Loussoi where Melampous healed the daughters of Proitos (see note to *PF* 37), or, more esoterically, to *Hemerasia*, "she who tames," the resulting etiological epithet Artemis acquired there (see Pausanias 8.7.8), or to "Sicyon," where Krebs had told Barker emphatically the cowgirls were not cured (see Letter to Sewtor Lowden, 26 October 1951). Whatever the case, it is important to note the hierarchical and psychological implications of this aspect of the first meeting and its tenacious longevity in Sewtor-Lowden's memory. The word *lusimeles*, "limb-loosener," is a descriptive epithet of the power of Eros to make a man or woman weak in the knees over another. Poets like Sappho, Archilochos, and Hedylos use it, but we cannot say with certitude if Ananios ever or never did. For "the favorite middle deponent," see *PF* 29a and note. Having spoken freely and possibly too frankly above, I leave to the scrutiny of others what Sewtor-Lowden's reference to "my *anagnorisis*," the Greek term for the "discovery" or "recognition" essential to a plot of complex action in a tragedy according to Aristotle in his

Poetics, 10–11, reveals about his sense of self. As he summons up his memory of the conditions of his assignation with Demetra, Sewtor-Lowden recalls the ruins of a church that had been partially constructed with fragments of capitals and whole drum sections of Doric columns, a common building practice, prominently exemplified by the twelfth-century church known as the Ayios Eleftherios next to the Metropolis of Athens several blocks west of Constitution Square, in which the stones from pagan temples integrated into the structure include one with what is thought to be the face of Marsyas sculpted upon it but reconceived hierotopically as that of John the Baptist. Such an interlocking of two different cultures, pagan and Christian, through the single language of stone building blocks, offers us a singular instantiation of the dynamics of religious syncretism, a word both Professor Stavrides and some of our dictionaries remind us originally denoted a union of Cretan parties against a common foe, which in this case would be the big *Nihilismus*. (This reminds me, though the analogy is obviously limited, of a papyrus fragment (#4922ab) Trajan Johnson reportedly kept in his office to show his visitors, who were frequent and many. The surviving two pieces of the fragment contain two texts, the earlier one being identified as a portion of the second book of Xenophon's *Cyropaedia*, and the second one, about four centuries later, being a Christian homily or a commentary on Exodus 14–15, in which the destruction of Pharaoh's army is described. Because the Christian text is written between the margins on the front and on the back, the papyrus has been designated as "reused" or "recycled," but I wonder if the military nature of the ancient Greek text does not propose a challenge to our ingenuity or propensity to meaningfully coordinate the constituents of any and all artifacts we inherit. At the least, it is rather astonishing to recognize that this passage of the *Cyropaedia*, 2.1.11, is also the source of the inscription on Krebs' card, for which see above, Letter to Sewtor-Lowden, 25 September 1951.) *Katheghitis Yermanos* would be "German Professor" and *aghoria*, "boys" in Greek, *Eine Ironie des Schicksals*, "an irony of fate" in German, and *adelphotis*, "brotherhood" in Greek. One wonders if Sewtor-Lowden became familiar with the three German terms, *Judenvernichtungsbefehl*, "order to exterminate the Jews," *Vernichtungskrieg*, "annihilation warfare," and *Sühnemassnahmen*, "atonement action," along with the Greek word for "guerrillas," *andartes*, and the acronym "ELAS," one of the two

Communist affiliated resistance forces, before or after he assumed his official duties with the Association of Martyred Towns. According to the reports of some of the thirteen male survivors of the execution and others who witnessed or participated in the reprisal action, which lasted no more than an hour, Commandant Tenner was methodically eating almonds from a paper bag throughout the event up until the moment he dropped the bag to the ground and raised his arm to order the machine gunning to commence. Before the slaughter, that tiny droplet in human history's enormous bucket of blood, he shelled and ate his almonds, for which he apparently had a great weakness, as he and his men marched their victims out of the town and up the hill, leaving a trail of shells and papery fragments along their route to the place where they would scatter the spent shells of their machine guns, the husks of Farmer Death's harvest. That Tasso and Vasso were there elicits Sewtor-Lowden's final Greek quotation, the closing words of the Muse's last grief-stricken speech over the death of her son, murdered by Odysseus and Diomedes, near the end of the *Rhesus* of Euripides, *O paidopoioi symphorai, ponoi broton*, "O disastrous childbearing, humanity's grief," which continues with the lines, "Whoever can reckon the good from the bad, / will choose to live childless, never to bear children to the grave" (980–82). This has the appearance of an intensely personal moment, though not so intense or unqualifiedly personal as to blunt the compulsion to offer an opinion on the nagging, unresolved issue of the play's attribution to Euripdes. Yet who is to say the reversal of position on the tragedy's authorship was not at least partially consequential to the experience of this most recent journey to Greece? As for the reference to "Die Fragmente der Ananius," was it to a working title Sewtor-Lowden found in the packet from Germany that Barker delivered to him, a phrase remembered from a conversation that had occurred decades before, or an invention of the moment?

Index Nominum

ANONYMOUS ALEXANDRIAN, THE

The Anonymous Alexandrian was just that, in the years following the flight out of the city by Aristarchos of Samothrace (c.217–145 BC) and most of Alexandria's scholars and intellectuals upon the accession of Ptolemy VIII in 145 BC. He was probably a pupil of Aristarchos, the great chief librarian of Alexandria and famous editor of Homer, Hesiod, Pindar and other poets, who succeeded his own teacher and accomplished chief librarian, Aristophanes of Byzantium (c.257–180 BC). Historians of the Alexandria Library often associate the name of the poet Kallimachos (c. 310–240 BC) with Aristarchos and Aristophanes, but we should remember that the renowned poet was never chief librarian but chief cataloguer, having been employed in that post by Ptolemy II (Philadelphus). Though his cataloging work earned him admiration, Kallimachos was passed over for the position of boss librarian in favor of Apollonius Rhodios (c.295–230 BC), the author of the *Argonautica* and his former pupil and bitter rival. That Aristarchos, who died on the island of Cyprus that same year, and so many others who were part of the city's celebrated creative and intellectual tradition departed in 145, has been charged to the recognition that life under the physically and morally gross Ptolemy VIII would have been intolerable to individuals of such preeminence, not to mention how dangerous it would have been to remain in Egypt for those who had opposed him during the earlier period of his rule (170–163). Such imputations may be further supported by noting that Ptolemy VIII's official royal titles, Euergetes (Benefactor) and Tryphon (Magnificent) were popularly reversed through the wordplay the ancients called *prosonomasia* to Kakegertes (Malefactor) and Physcon (Potbelly or Fatso), respectively, the latter jesting title being by far the most commonly and longest held among his subjects and subsequently by historians, for the murderous and vengeful—it goes without saying, lustful—Ptolemy exhibited an inordinate fondness for gauzy garments, through which he flaunted his disgusting corpulence. So the return of Physcon to Memphis as Pharaoh in 145 (this second reign ended with his death in 116) precipitated a voluntary exodus of scholars and intellectuals, whose number swelled through his own decrees of expulsion against Jews and other undesirables. The fortuitous cultural expansion that resulted from this emigration of eminent Alexandrians throughout the Hellenistic world to the great benefit of its Roman conquerors would have been completely unexpected by the likes of Ptolemy VIII, whose lack of anticipation of which could only be matched by his indifference to its significance. Like the tiny balls of fire and sparks scattered by an exploding Roman candle, the departing literati inseminated the entire Mediterranean with new poetic light. By remaining home, whether out of bravery or necessity, the Anonymous Alexandrian kept alive for a little longer the embers of the once great fire of scholarship that had blazed in his city.

BARKER, JONATHAN

Jonathan Barker was born on February 29, 1924, in Greenwich, England, the only child of Eric, a technician at the Royal Conservatory, and Maud Barker, both of whom died within several days of each other in 1936 as a result of injuries sustained as passengers in an automobile accident. He was taken in by his maternal grandparents, Nathan and Barbara Marshall of Canterbury, who made every sacrifice possible to provide him with excellent schooling and a university education. By the time he was doing his graduate studies in Greek with Sir Michael Sewtor-Lowden at Cambridge in the middle nineteen-fifties they had both passed away and, as his father's parents had divorced when he was a child and occupied little or no place of significance in his life, he was on his own. Upon completion of his dissertation, "Minacious Discourse: Warrior Speech in Homer's *Iliad*," he accepted a position at St. Thomas's School Harpenden in 1952, where he remained until his death as the result of a major stroke on February 29, 1984. His widow, Wink, née Cavanaugh, the school librarian, whom he married in 1979, said, "Jack often predicted he would die, as he was born, in a Leap Year, but never went so far as to prognosticate his demise on the supernumerary day of his birth." After the death of Sir Michael Sewtor-Lowden in 1975, he made inquiries at the law firm of Burke, Potter, and Quimby, the trustees of Sir Michael's estate, concerning the papers related to the preparation of the edition of the poems of Ananios of Kleitor, including those that Sewtor-Lowden had received from the German scholar Anastas Krebs, in connection with an essay he was planning to write on the subject of his former mentor's accomplishments as a textual editor. Mr. Keith Quimby, the firm member to whom the execution of the literary and scholarly materials in the estate have been entrusted, regretfully informed him that all such papers pertaining to the edition of Ananios were not to be found among the Sewtor-Lowden archival collections. Indeed, according to Professor Hugh Sydle, whom Mr. Quimby, as a courtesy to Barker, had consulted on the subject, all of Sir Michael's working papers, printer's proofs, etc. relevant to the Ananios edition are missing—all, that is, except for the singular and notorious piece of paper that had made its way somehow into the Gray/ Sewtor-Lowden Euripides files and mysteriously emerged to play its causative role in the unfortunate accident that befell Sir Michael that fatal day. Mrs. Barker, who later came across her husband's correspondence with Quimby about this matter among his papers, acknowledges that "Jack was profoundly disappointed by 'this twist of fate—or the facts,' as he put it," and had confided to her once that his feelings about the entire disturbing episode involving Krebs, Sewtor-Lowden, and himself with the poems of Ananios revived some turbulent emotions he experienced as a boy when he was severely disciplined for, and subsequently prohibited from, playing on his favorite mound on the Greenwich grounds, it being the covered over well once used by John Flamsteed (1646–1719), the founder of the Observatory and first Astronomer Royal, for his daylight observations. Out of concern for her husband's emotional state, Mrs. Barker was reluctant to pursue the significance of this troubling connection for him. Instead, she worked diligently with him on a plan to prepare his dissertation for publication and to find an appropriate publisher to which to submit it.

GIESING, WILHELM

The son of a famous historian and papyrologist, Professor Armin Giesing of Heidelberg University, Wilhelm was born in that city on November 9, 1886 (d. Munich, March 11, 1962). Despite his father's persistent urging that he concentrate his studies in the fields of Greek paleography and papyrology, Wilhelm was drawn to the then newly burgeoning field of comparative literary history and, to his father's chagrin, chose Freiburg for his university studies, where he remained for several years on the faculty. One of the group of younger teachers and students who strongly supported the policies of the newly appointed rector of the university, Martin Heidegger, in the early nineteen thirties, Giesing later lost his position at Freiburg and eventually gained an appointment at the Ludwig-Maximillians-Universität of Munich, quite possibly with the help of Professor Anastas Krebs, whom he had known since adolescence in a relationship that endured the vicissitudes of several emotionally charged sea changes. His best-known work and only book is his exploration of the influence of the civilization of antiquity on the writings of Johann Wolfgang von Goethe, *Goethe und die Antike*, published in 1934.

KOSMAS LOGOTHETES

Floruit the middle of the sixth century AD during the reign of the Emperor Justinian (527–565). Piecing together what little is known about this Kosmas, we find ourselves constructing a portrait of a man who may well have participated in the lewd theatrical performances staged by Theodora before she married Justinian and eventually became Empress. It is possible that, like her, he was born on the island of Cyprus and came to Constantinople as a youngster. He obviously enjoyed the status as one of her favorites, for after her surprising upwardly mobile marriage he followed her to the palace and the women's apartments therein, in which he was employed as one of the cooks. It was probably there in the *gynaikonitis* that he took up the study of poetry and rhetoric, there being no shortage of good books in that venue. After the death of Theodora in 548, he continued to enjoy good fortune in the great city, for Justinian granted him an appointment as *logothetes*, one of the most sought after and difficult to obtain posts in the imperial administration. As agents of the treasury and paymasters to the army, the *logothetai* were notorious for their oppressive and corrupt self-serving conduct in the name of the Emperor and the Empire. Like those who had preceded and those who have succeeded him in similar trajectories of career as take one out of the world of study and elevate him into what appears to be the superior world of administrative operations, Kosmas, upon becoming "the Logothete" [*o logothetes*], seems to have abandoned his pious pursuit of literary recipes for rhetoric and embraced the opportunities for advancement and enrichment offered by his new post. About the rest of his life, we know little that is definite, though some scholars of the period claim to have examined documents which mention two men named Kosmas, one of whom is said to have left the service of Justinian as *logothetes* upon the Emperor's death in 565 and entered a monastery, and the other of whom it was recorded that he was murdered by an outraged, revengeful soldier in the imperial army who believed the paymaster had levied penalties against him simply for being from Greece. An exit resulting from foul play, such as this latter account provides, seems most appropriate and poetically, if not rhetorically, just, considering the shameless nature of the licentious public displays in which he took part after his entrance earlier in the century into the sensuously pulsating life of Constantine's city.

Nothing, outside of the work itself, is known about the conditions under which Kosmas Logothetes composed his *Recipes for Rhetoric* [ΣΥΝΤΑΓΑΙ ΠΕΡΙ ΤΗΣ ΡΗΤΟΡΙΚΗΣ] (*Syntagai peri tes Rhetorikes*). That he was not yet *logothetes* but still cook and rhetorician when he wrote it we know from his references to himself in those capacities in the text as *mageiros* and *rhetor*. His recognition of authorship, along with publication, must have come during the later part of his career as an official of the government, just as the actual research and writing of the work most likely occurred during the previous twenty or more years he spent in the palace. (There is no supporting evidence anywhere for the notion that before being allowed to serve in the palace Kosmas was forced to become a eunuch, a condition that would most certainly have cut off his chances of being appointed as *logothetes*.) When he wasn't involved in the preparation of dishes for Theodora and her retinue of attendants and eunuchs, who spent much of the time between meals engaged in buffoonery and luxurious indolence, he indulged his interest in the amatory verse of the ancients under the cover of pursuing examples of the rhetorical arts that would provide literary instruction for his readers at the same time as it offered them lessons in Christian morality, the purported benefactions behind which he concealed his true intentions, which, in my perhaps too harsh view, were rooted entirely in his prurient nature. Among the sources to which he had access there must have been something akin to what we call and know as *The Greek Anthology*, for among the poets he holds up to his sanctimonious scorn are his contemporaries Paulos Silentiarius and Maximos Hypatos (the Consul), both figures of greater importance than he in the imperial court and both good Christians, their ability to write poems in successful emulation of the finest examples in the tradition of their pagan predecessors notwithstanding. It appears that in one of these sources (not

The Greek Anthology in any of its serial incarnations known to posterity) the erroneous confusion between Ananios of Kleitor and the sixth century iambic poet of the same name occurs, as the fourth quotation in Kosmas' discussion of *zeugma* is identical to one of the handful of fragments now attributed with certainty to the earlier iambographer.

KREBS, ANASTAS

Anastas Krebs, who was born on Easter Sunday, March 25, 1883, in Darmstadt, Germany, was a classicist on the faculty of the Ludwig-Maximilians-Universität, Munich, from 1919 until his death during a trip to Greece on December 13, 1951. Though he became well known for his highly original scholarship on ancient Greek military history and warfare, Krebs was always a devoted student of the poetry of classical antiquity, undoubtedly the result of a passionate interest in poetry of all kinds, which had begun in childhood and remained with him for his entire life. He worked for some years locating and gathering textual sources for what would have been a pioneering edition of the poems of Ananios of Kleitor, an early fourth century poet about whom little was known other than the fact that he shared the name Ananios with a minor sixth century iambic poet of unknown geographical provenance whose handful of fragments and testimonials associate, if not at times confuse, him with the better known iambographer Hipponax. Working rather generally at first in the Bayerische Staatsbibliothek of Munich with various papyri of the second century BC pertaining to several poets, including Ananios, from the Myrsinus archive in Philadelphia (Darb-el-Gerza), Krebs then moved on serendipitously to consult with greater specificity papyrus fragments collected in Berlin, London, and Oxford from various other sites in the Fayyûm area along the upper Nile. For it was during research trips to the libraries of those cities before the first World War, when he was seeking information related to the Battle of the Stockade outside Corinth in 393 BC, that he came across papyrus rolls and fragments containing verse he was convinced was written by Ananios of Kleitor. Recalling his earlier interest in the poet, Krebs diverted some of the attention he had reserved for his announced attempt to make better sense than hitherto of the indecisive battle fought between the long walls of Corinth that had pitted Spartans, Sicyonians, and Corinthian oligarchs against Argives, Athenians, and Corinthian democrats to an effort to extend our knowledge of the poetic productivity of Ananios. It is also possible that the scattered references to the poet in the literary remains of antiquity, including the supposition, based on the remarks of an early commentator, that the poet had spent considerable time in Corinth, particularly as a regular visitor to the Temple of Aphrodite, captivated the imagination of the young scholar, who was quickly earning a reputation for his enthusiastic and impressionable nature. His senior scholars and colleagues, including his mentor, the redoubtable Armin Giesing, apparently discouraged Krebs from continuing this work, urging him instead to complete his first book, a radical reconsideration of the events surrounding the battle of the stockade during the Corinthian War, which he dutifully did, publishing it finally under the title *Der korinthische Krieg: Versuch einer Neubewertung* in 1920. Yet, in the midst of conducting the kind of research in military history and theory for which Krebs is widely recognized, he persisted in the pursuit of his poet's edition, fighting the silence of his fellow scholars with his own silent, subterranean, as it were, labors, which even involved attempts to reconstruct to their totality some of the poems from diverse lacunose sources. He also journeyed to Greece more than once, visiting in particular ancient Corinth and the sparse ruins of Kleitor in the province of Kalavryta in the northwestern Peloponnesian Prefecture of Achaia. It was there that he met the young Michael Sewtor-Lowden, a classicist from Cambridge University, in 1927, inaugurating an affiliation that may well have exceeded the limits of professional formality, though its character through the years proved to be more sporadic than constant. Nevertheless, it was into Sewtor-Lowden's hands that all of Krebs' Ananios work fell shortly before the German scholar's death, and eight years later, in 1960, *The Poems of Ananius of Clitor: An Authoritative Edition Compiled and Annotated, with an Introduction by Sir Michael Sewtor-Lowden* appeared under the imprint of William Grossmann, Ltd. of London.

The son of Justus Krebs, a member of the engineering faculty at Darmstadt's well-known technical university, and Hannah Jahr, an accomplished artist whose original paintings in the manner of the experimental new styles attracted notable attention beyond the boundaries of the state of Hesse, young Anastas, along with his slightly older sister Ursula, was raised in a household whose daily routines were suffused with the markings of culture and science. It is noteworthy that both Justus and Hannah's families traced lineal descent from a common ancestor, the eighteenth-century composer and organist Johann Ludwig Krebs. Indicative of his parents' notable prominence in the city are the facts that his father enjoyed an assignment in the building in 1898–99 of the famous Russian Church commissioned by Tsar Nicholas II in honor of Tsarina Alexandra, who was born in Darmstadt; while his mother, to whom he was much more deeply attached, was involved in the establishment of the city's new artists' colony in the Mathildenhöhe sponsored by the grand duke Ernst Ludwig. By the time he was twelve, Anastas had acquired a reputation for being an intense, impulsive, and unpredictable youth, an exceptional and unique *Muttersöhnchen*, control over whom resided almost exclusively in his mother, whose indoctrinations of her son in the values of radical art and writing, supplemented by a strenuous literary upbringing which involved the memorization and spontaneous recitation of poetry in staggering proportions, only compromised the ameliorating effects of her resolute maternal influence upon his intractable spirit. Desperate to reform his son and point him in the direction of a useful career, Justus conferred with his brother Max, the father of the future General Hans Krebs, Hitler's last chief of staff, and decided to send Anastas to the Realschule in Linz, Austria, where he would engage his wits in the study of science preparatory to a calling in technology and engineering. Anastas, with the uncompromising support of his mother, in whose diaries and letters much of this family history is recorded, violently opposed this plan. Fighting husband and father as comrades-in-arms, mother and son finally prevailed and, luckily, Anastas was not sent off to Linz, where he might have been exposed, as many boys of his generation were, to the rabid *Völkisch* nationalism of history master Leopold Pötsch. Instead, as a concession to her husband's unwavering demand that their son be subjected to some form of academic discipline, Hannah arranged for him to attend the Gymnasium in Heidelberg, living at the home of one of her childhood friends, Armin Giesing, the aforementioned renowned scholar of non-literary papyri and ostraca, who was a professor of ancient history and classical languages at the university there. Giesing, who had a boy of his own around the same age, promised his friend he would treat her son as his own, and indeed it was from Giesing that Krebs learned to take his classical schooling with the utmost seriousness, leading him eventually to his matriculation at Heidelberg and his university living, a "gift" Krebs resolved to pass along to his nephew, his sister Ursula's son, Siegfried Wenzel-Schott, who, instead, was to become one of the estimated fifty million individuals who perished in World War II.

SEWTOR-LOWDEN, SIR MICHAEL

Born in Northampton, England, on July 14, 1900, into one of the city's prominent shoe manufacturing families, young Michael avoided following in his forbears' footsteps by devoting himself single-mindedly to the study of classical languages and literature, especially Greek. He spent his entire career as student and faculty at Cambridge, "wafted by a westerly breeze from home to University," as he used to say, Cambridge being situated a short distance due east of Northampton. A student of the renowned scholar Arnold Gray, who attained a reputation as one of the world's greatest authorities on Euripides without ever publishing a single word of his life-long work about the tragedian, young Sewtor-Lowden took his D. Litt. in 1926, and after a year and a half of travel financed by his father and younger brother, settled into his appointment at Kythe College, of which he eventually became master. There is no need to list his numerous publications here; suffice it to say the countless articles and notes in scholarly journals, monographs, and editions, not to mention his lecture tours and BBC programs, earned him the reputation that occasioned his being knighted in the year 1947 by King George VI. It was soon after this honor had been conferred upon him that he met King Paul and Queen Frederika of Greece, who, along with the British crown and government, sponsored Sir Michael's appointment to the governing board of the International Association of Martyred Towns. The rate of his scholarly productivity diminished during the latter years of his career, though he continued to mentor doctoral students until his death. He never completed the study of Euripides based on the unpublished writings of the by then late Arnold Gray, which was announced by its prospective publisher as "a major collaboration of scholarly minds." Sewtor-Lowden himself has been recorded as saying, at a banquet in his honor during the last days of his life, "I fear that, as we now all know, I shall not fulfill my promise to bring to term dear, departed, dead Graysie's gift of his Euripides to me." His last significant publication was the edition of the poems of Ananios of Kleitor, which appeared in 1960.

The expected cause of death of Sir Michael Sewtor-Lowden, who was suffering at the time from leukemia with a prognosis of a few months to live at the most, was preempted on May 3, 1975, by an accidental fall through his second story study window to the stone path below. According to the only witness, his former student Hugh Sydle, who had come to Cambridge from the United States for the honorific banquet and to discuss his assuming the responsibility of preparing the Gray and Sewtor-Lowden Euripides papers and manuscripts for publication, Sir Michael was sitting on the window seat before the fully opened single-sash casement window, where Professor Sydle had helped him move several minutes earlier. Sydle was standing behind Sewtor-Lowden's desk, several feet away, sorting through Gray's notebooks while Sir Michael was examining variously sized loose sheets of paper that had been gathered into a manila folder. His last words were, "How did this get in here?" as he examined and then set down a small piece of paper on to the seat cushion in front of him. He no sooner had put it down than a sudden breeze lifted it off the cushion and conveyed it with a light upward, perverse little twist into the air outside the window. As if by reflex, Sir Michael lunged with left arm outstretched towards the floating fragment of paper, which he—to Sydle's and his own momentary amazement—captured, but, losing his balance, he began to fall through the window. His only hope, which he seemed to recognize instinctively, was to grab hold of a bough of an old elm tree next to the building, but the strength of his right arm and hand was not equal to the task. Sydle's rush around the wide desk and across the room was not in time, and, after calling out for help at the window, hurried down to his fallen mentor. Though Sir Michael survived the fall, in which he broke both hips and sustained a concussion, he never regained consciousness and passed away quietly a few hours later.

During his statement at the inquest, according to the local newspaper report, Sydle was asked to explain the nature of the piece of paper that had precipitated this tragic event. Still tightly clutched in Sir Michael's left hand when the medics arrived and eventually filed with the coroner's official report of finding as "death by accident," it was shown to Professor Sydle for decipherment of what appeared to be a line of several words in Greek with a number of punctuation marks and typographical symbols interspersed and a phrase in German below them. It was, Sydle stated, most likely a transcription of a verse of Greek poetry, found on a fragment of papyrus, by the ancient Greek poet Ananios of Kleitor, whose works the deceased had edited some years earlier; the German phrase identified the source as a small strip of mummy cartonnage from Aphroditopolis (Atfieh) on the east bank of the Nile in the Fayyûm region of Egypt. When asked to put it into English for the record, Sydle thought for a moment and said, "It is quite difficult to translate under these conditions. The best I can do is that some person hopes to come to—rather to become like a Corinthian."

SYDLE, HUGH

Though every generation of Sydles, descendants of an adventurous German ancestor (Kurt Seidel), who had emigrated to England in the 18th century from the city of Bremen, had worked in the cutlery industry of Sheffield, Hugh (b. March 18, 1925), the youngest child of a large family, was encouraged by his elders to seek a professional life. After completing his undergraduate studies at Sheffield University, Sydle moved up to Cambridge, where his studies were primarily guided by the eminent Sir Michael Sewtor-Lowden, who directed his dissertation, "Euripides and the Politics of Athenian Festival Drama Competitions," which he completed in 1951. After brief periods of employment during his student days in Cambridge at the Joint Association of Classical Teachers and the International Biographical Centre, he worked for a few months in London in the acquisitions department of the publishing house of William Grossmann. In the fall of 1952, he moved to the Chicago area of the United States when he was offered a tenure-track assistant professorship in the department of Classics at the State University of Illinois at Winnetka. Remaining at SUIW for the next four and a half decades, Dr. Sydle assisted Professor Joseph Fisher in the editing of *The Review of Classical Studies*, a prominent journal in the field published by their department, and eventually rose to its editorship, and, shortly thereafter, to the department chairmanship upon Fisher's retirement in 1960. He played a major role in the fund-raising campaign in the Chicago metropolitan area, especially in the communities on the western shore of Lake Michigan from Skokie to Waukegan, for the endowment of the Fylfot Professorship of Classics, and was named as the new chair's first professor. Though Sir Michael Sewtor-Lowden had invited Sydle to assist him in preparing the edition of the poems of Ananios of Kleitor, which was published by William Grossmann, Ltd. in 1960, it appears that Sydle either declined the offer or that it was withdrawn. He has not yet completed the work on Euripides by Arnold Gray and Sewtor-Lowden that was entrusted to him at the time of Sir Michael's fatal accident in 1975. He did publish a major article, however, in the issue of *RCS* dedicated to him upon his retirement in 1985, "Unconventional Conventionality: Subversion as Normative Strategy in Euripides." This article, the writing of which Sydle described at the ceremony staged by the president of SUIW in his honor as "a ripping, riveting experience," has been hailed by a younger generation of classicists as "a seminal contribution to the multi-acculturation of the classics discipline." Not surprisingly, his hitherto and still unpublished dissertation has been recently referred to as "a work ahead of its time in its pre-post-modern politicized contextualizations of Greek drama events."

After his retirement, Professor Sydle and his wife Annette have remained in Winnetka, though he makes annual journeys abroad to Sheffield and Cambridge. He and his wife have a daughter, Melanie, who pursues a notable specialized practice in bovine and other large animal veterinarian medicine near Eau Claire, Wisconsin.

THEONAEUS
Floruit the early third century AD in and around Athens and the island of Aegina, though he was probably born in Corinth. His reputation rests solely upon his authorship of a long anthological work whose title, *Games for Dinnertime* (ΔΕΙΠΝΟΠΑΙΔΕΙΑΙ [*Deipnopaideiai*]), suggests dinners serving simultaneously as ludic courses of instruction as well as an entertaining pastime. Because the work, a good two-thirds of which it is estimated has survived, was primarily concerned with poetry and poets, it stands as an invaluable source of the verse of Ananios of Kleitor. Unlike all of us who have followed him, the writer—perhaps compiler would be the more precise description—of *Games for Dinnertime* enjoyed the benefit of the study by Chamaemelon of Patrae on Achaian and Arcadian poets, a work now lost, along with its very title, but well attested by the mentions of numerous authors from the second and first centuries BC down to Theonaeus himself, who is not only the last of its

readers to cite it but also the only extant writer to quote and paraphrase from it on the subject of Ananios. The evidence points to a time of composition for Chamaemelon's book of approximately one hundred years after the prime of Ananios' career, that is to say, about 240–230 BC. Thus, by virtue of its chronological proximity to the lifetime of Ananios and its outliving itself through the enterprising intertextual efforts of Theonaeus, Chamaemelon's lost work is possessed of a special, albeit apparitional, status as an authority on the poet from Kleitor. It would be risky, however, to assume that Theonaeus did not have other avenues of access to the poetry of Ananios, for he quotes a number of passages without attribution to Chamaemelon, a practice whose integrity we have no reason to question. While we cannot say for certain that the missing parts of *Games for Dinnertime* did not contain more passages from Ananios or within quotations from Chamaemelon, we can be reasonably sure, thanks to the scholarship of Traianos Giannakopoulos (later Trajan Johnson) that historical persons of Theonaeus' acquaintance furnished the small circle of speakers who populate its lively and often amusing scenes of literary conversation.

THEOPHANES

Floruit the middle of the eleventh century. Though he referred to himself as "Father of the Holy Hermitage," he was generally known as "the Mad Monk of the Morea." Probably born early in the century in Constantinople during the reign of Basil II (the Bulgar Slayer), Theophanes was ordained in the priesthood and became attached to the great house of Monomachos. After the brief reign of Basil's hedonistic brother Constantine VIII as Emperor of Byzantium, the tumultuous period of history inaugurated by the succession of his daughter Zoë Porphyrogenita began in the year 1028, resulting in events that had a profound effect upon Theophanes. After Zoë's handsome and epilectic lover Michael, with whom she had probably poisoned her first husband Romanos III (Argyros), joined her on the throne as Michael IV (the Paphlagonian), he promptly banished Constantine Monomachos, not only because he was related by marriage to the late Romanos, but also, as future events proved, somewhat presciently, because he regarded him as an old rival for the affections of the Basilissa. Theophanes went into exile with his lord to Mytilene on the island of Lesbos but did not return to Constantinople with him several years later. How Theophanes ended up in the Peloponnese, seven kilometers southwest of present day Kalavryta, at a small monastery (founded in 961) which would become centuries later the great Ayia Lavra, celebrated as the site at which the War of Independence began in 1821, remains as much a mystery to historians as the fact that he did not return to Constantinople with Monomachos when Zoë recalled him to marry and serve with her as Emperor (the fourth man to do so) in 1042 remains a certainty. Spending the rest of his life at the monastery, when he wasn't wandering about the area, Theophanes, according to his own testimony, preached about the evils of the times, past and present, and, when the spirit moved him, played the prophet as well, to whomever or whatever, animate and inanimate, he believed could hear him. The immoral and destructive reign of Zoë, quite understandably, was one of his favorite topics, as was her failure to produce an heir, which was, of course, no wonder (to us if not to him) since the first of her four marriages, to Romanos Argyros, did not occur until she was forty-eight years old. He was equally passionate, if not terribly coherent, in his views about the Great Schism of 1054, for which he blamed Zoë, though it occurred four years after her death and was hardly caused by the actions and intrigues of a vain and capricious woman but rather by the growing intensity of long term political and religious conflicts between East and West which culminated in the break provoked by the mutual accusations and excommunications pronounced by the Patriarch, Michael Cerularios, and Pope Leo IX and his papal legates to Byzantium. Theophanes recorded these and other views in a book he called *The Holy Book of Accounts* [TO IEPON ΓΡΑΜΜΑΤΕΙΟΝ (*To Hieron Grammateion*)], a work which, ironically, was deposited in the library of the Vatican, conveyed there with other manuscripts taken from the hermitage, after a series of earthquakes, by agents of the houses of Othon de Tournay and Guillaume de Villehardouin during the late thirteenth century. Among those manuscripts may have been an anthology of Greek poetry, now apparently lost, which Theophanes had probably brought with him into exile, for he shows familiarity in his writing with many ancient poets, including Ananios of Kleitor, though it appears he or his source confused Ananios with the earlier iambic poet of the same name from the sixth century.

A Note on Sources

A full bibliographic record of the groundwork of sources from which the poetry of Ananios and its reception originates would exceed not only the power of memory to encompass it but also the number of pages the most well-meaning and accommodating of publishers could possibly allot to it. The following list of titles, however, acknowledges several works as having played special and unique, though distinctly different, roles in the narrative conveyance of the Greek poet's retrieval: James Davidson, *Courtesans and Fishcakes: The Consuming Passions of Classical Athens* (Thomas Dunne, 1998); Kathleen Freeman, *Greek City States* (Norton, 1950); Herbert Kubly, *Gods and Heroes* (Doubleday, 1969); Mark Mazower, *Inside Hitler's Greece: The Experience of Occupation 1941–44* (Yale University Press, 1993); E. G. Turner, *Greek Papyri, An Introduction* (Clarendon Press, Oxford, 1968); Herbert C. Youtie, "The Papyrologist: Artificer of Fact," *Greek, Roman and Byzantine Studies*, Vol. 4 (1963), 19–32; and almost everything I could lay my hands on by the late lamented Charles Segal. Finally, I thank Karin Schutjer for providing the title of a 1920 German scholarly work that would likely be described today as a "counterintuitive interpretation" of the events related to the Battle of the Stockade outside Corinth in the early fourth-century BC.

—G. E.

The Author

George Economou was born in Great Falls, Montana, and was educated at Colgate and Columbia Universities. Named twice as Fellow in Poetry by the National Endowment for the Humanities, he has also held fellowships from the Rockefeller Foundation and the American Council of Learned Societies. He retired as Professor Emeritus of English after forty-one years of teaching, the last seventeen of which were at the University of Oklahoma. He lives in Philadelphia and Wellfleet, Massachusetts.

Printed in the United States
153281LV00001B/205/P